Unit Assessments

www.mheonline.com/readingwonders

Send all inquiries to:
McGraw-Hill Education
Two Penn Plaza
New York, New York 10121

ISBN: 978-0-07-677055-7
MHID: 0-07-677055-9

Printed in the United States of America.

1 2 3 4 5 6 7 8 9 RHR 20 19 18 17 16 15

A

Table of Contents

Teacher Introduction

Unit Assessments

The *Unit Assessments* component is an integral part of the complete assessment program aligned with *Reading Wonders* and state standards.

Purpose

This component reports on the outcome of student learning. As students complete each unit of the reading program, they will be assessed on their understanding of key instructional content and their ability to write to source texts/stimuli. The results serve as a summative assessment by providing a status of current achievement in relation to student progress through the curriculum. The results of the assessments can be used to inform subsequent instruction, aid in making leveling and grouping decisions, and point toward areas in need of reteaching or remediation.

Focus

Unit Assessments focuses on key areas of English Language Arts—comprehension of literature and informational text, vocabulary acquisition and use, command of the conventions of the English language, and genre writing in response to sources.

Each unit assessment also provides students familiarity with the item types, the test approaches, and the increased rigor associated with the advances in high-stakes assessment, such as the *Smarter Balanced Assessment Consortium* (SBAC) summative assessment system.

Test Administration

Each unit assessment should be administered once the instruction for the specific unit is completed. Make copies of the unit assessment for the class. You will need copies of the Answer Key pages that feature the scoring tables for each student taking the assessment. These tables provide a place to list student scores. The data from each unit assessment charts student progress and underscores strengths and weaknesses.

This component is the pencil-and-paper version of the assessment. You can administer the online version of the test, which allows for tech-enabled and tech-enhanced item functionality.

NOTE: Due to time constraints, you may wish to administer the unit assessment over multiple days. For example, students can complete Questions 1–31 on the first day and complete the Performance Task on another. For planning purposes, the recommended time for each task is 90–100 minutes over two back-to-back sessions. During the first session, provide students 30–40 minutes to read the stimulus materials and answer the research questions. During the second session, provide students 60–70 minutes for planning, writing, and editing their responses. If desired, provide students a short break between sessions. If you decide to break-up administration by assessment sections, please remember to withhold those sections of the test students are not completing to ensure test validity.

#21 in each assessment is focused on students comparing texts/writing across texts. This is a continuation of the optional activity featured in *Weekly Assessments,* and it provides valuable practice for the type of critical thinking and writing required in performance-based assessments. If you feel students have adequate exposure to this writing performance in the tasks and removing the item will reduce test administration time, you can decide not to administer item #21 and remove that page from the test packet. Deleting the item will result in a 50-point skill test; note this deletion in your scoring tables.

Teacher Introduction

After each student has a copy of the assessment, provide a version of the following directions:

Say: *Write your name and the date on the question pages for this assessment.* (When students are finished, continue with the directions.) *You will read four texts and answer questions about them. In the next part of the test, you will read drafts and/or passages. You will revise these or edit for the correct grammar, mechanics, and usage. In the final part of the test, you will read sources, answer questions about them, and write a response based on the assignment you will find, an assignment that will ask you to use those sources in your writing.*

Read each part of the test carefully. For multiple-choice items, completely fill in the circle next to the correct answer or answers. For items that ask you to write on the page, look carefully at the directions to answer the question. You may be asked to match items, circle or underline choices, complete a chart, or place details in order. For constructed response items, write your response on the lines provided. For the performance tasks, write your response to the assignment on clean sheets of paper. When you have completed the assessment, put your pencil down and turn the pages over. You may begin now.

Answer procedural questions during the assessment, but do not provide any assistance on the items or selections. Have extra paper on hand for students to use for their task responses. After the class has completed the assessment, ask students to verify that their names and the date are written on the necessary pages.

Assessment Items

Unit assessments feature the following item types—selected response (SR), multiple selected response (MSR), evidence-based selected response (EBSR), constructed response (CR), technology-enhanced items (TE), and extended constructed response (ECR). (Please note that the print versions of TE items are available in this component; the full functionality of the items is available only through the online assessment.) This variety of item types provides multiple methods of assessing student understanding, allows for deeper investigation into skills and strategies, and provides students an opportunity to become familiar with the kinds of questions they will encounter in state-mandated summative assessments.

Performance Tasks

Each unit features a Performance Task (PT) assessment in a previously-taught genre. Students will complete two examples of each type by the end of the year.

The task types are:

- Informational
  - Students generate a thesis based on the sources and use information from the sources to explain this thesis.
- Narrative
  - Students craft a narrative using information from the sources.
- Opinion
  - Students analyze the ideas in sources and make a claim that they support using the sources.

Each PT assesses standards that address comprehension, research skills, genre writing, and the use of standard English language conventions (ELC). The stimulus texts and research questions in each task build toward the goal of the final writing topic.

Teacher Introduction

Overview

- Students will read four texts in each assessment and respond to items focusing on Comprehension Skills, Literary Elements, Text Features, and Vocabulary Strategies. These items assess the ability to access meaning from the text and demonstrate understanding of unknown and multiple-meaning words and phrases.
- Students will then read a draft that requires corrections or clarifications to its use of the conventions of standard English language and/or complete a cloze passage that requires correct usage identification.
- Students are then presented with a Performance Task assignment.

Each test item in *Unit Assessments* (as well as in weekly and benchmark assessments) has a Depth of Knowledge (DOK) level assigned to it.

DOK 1 in vocabulary involves students using word parts (affixes, roots, and so on) to determine the meaning of an unknown word or non-contextual items assessing synonym/antonym and multiple-meaning words.

DOK 2 in vocabulary involves students using context to determine the meaning of an unknown word and dealing with figurative language in context.

DOK 1 in comprehension involves students identifying/locating information in the text.

DOK 2 in comprehension involves students analyzing text structures/story elements.

DOK 3 in comprehension involves students making inferences using text evidence and analyzing author's craft.

DOK 4 in comprehension involves using multiple stimulus texts and writing across texts.

DOK 1 in ELC/PTs involves students editing to fix errors.

DOK 2 in ELC/PTs involves students revising and planning writing or investigating sources.

DOK 3 and *DOK 4* in ELC/PTs involve research and student full-writes.

Each unit assessment features four "Cold Reads" on which the comprehension and vocabulary assessment items are based. These selections reflect the unit theme to support the focus of the classroom instruction. Texts fall within the Lexile band 740L–940L. Complexity on this quantitative measure grows throughout the units, unless a qualitative measure supports text placement outside a lockstep Lexile continuum.

Comprehension

Comprehension items in each unit assess student understanding of the text through the use of the Comprehension Skills, Literary Elements, and Text Features.

Vocabulary

Vocabulary items ask students to demonstrate the ability to uncover the meanings of unknown and multiple-meaning words and phrases using Vocabulary Strategies.

English Language Conventions

A total of ten items in each unit ask students to demonstrate their command of the conventions of standard English.

Performance Task

Students complete one task per unit, the final result being a written product in the specified task genre.

Teacher Introduction

Scoring

Use the scoring tables to assign final unit assessment scores. Each part of an EBSR is worth 1 point; MSR and TECR items should be answered correctly in full, though you may choose to provide partial credit.

For written responses, use the correct response parameters provided in the Answer Key and the scoring rubrics listed below to assign a score. Responses that show a complete lack of understanding or are left blank should be given a *0*.

Short Response Score: 2

The response is well-crafted and concise and shows a thorough understanding of the underlying skill. Appropriate text evidence is used to answer the question.

Short Response Score: 1

The response shows partial understanding of the underlying skill. Text evidence is featured, though examples are too general.

Extended Response Score: 4

- The student understands the question/prompt and responds suitably using the appropriate text evidence from the selection or selections.
- The response is an acceptably complete answer to the question/prompt.
- The organization of the response is meaningful.
- The response stays on topic; ideas are linked to one another with effective transitions.
- The response has correct spelling, grammar, usage, and mechanics.

Extended Response Score: 3

- The student understands the question/prompt and responds suitably using the appropriate text evidence from the selection or selections.
- The response is a somewhat complete answer to the question/prompt.
- The organization of the response is somewhat meaningful.
- The response maintains focus; ideas are linked to one another.
- The response has occasional errors in spelling, grammar, usage, and mechanics.

Extended Response Score: 2

- The student has partial understanding of the question/prompt and uses some text evidence.
- The response is an incomplete answer to the question/prompt.
- The organization of the response is weak.
- The writing is careless; contains extraneous information and ineffective transitions.
- The response requires effort to read easily.
- The response has noticeable errors in spelling, grammar, usage, and mechanics.

Extended Response Score: 1

- The student has minimal understanding of the question/prompt and uses little to no appropriate text evidence.
- The response is a barely acceptable answer to the question/prompt.
- The response lacks organization.
- The writing is erratic with little focus; ideas are not connected to each other.
- The response is difficult to follow.
- The response has frequent errors in spelling, grammar, usage, and mechanics.

Teacher Introduction

Use the rubrics to score the task holistically on a 10-point scale:
4 points for purpose/organization [P/O]; 4 points for evidence/elaboration [E/E] or development/elaboration [D/E]; and 2 points for English language conventions [C]

Unscorable or **Zero** responses are unrelated to the topic, illegible, contain little or no writing, or show little to no command of the conventions of standard English.

INFORMATIVE PERFORMANCE TASK SCORING RUBRIC

Score	Purpose/Organization	Evidence/Elaboration	Conventions
4	• **effective** organizational structure • clear statement of main idea based on purpose, audience, task • consistent use of various transitions • logical progression of ideas	• **convincing** support for main idea; **effective** use of sources • integrates comprehensive evidence from sources • relevant references • effective use of elaboration • audience-appropriate domain-specific vocabulary	
3	• **evident** organizational structure • adequate statement of main idea based on purpose, audience, task • adequate, somewhat varied use of transitions • adequate progression of ideas	• **adequate** support for main idea; **adequate** use of sources • some integration of evidence from sources • references may be general • adequate use of some elaboration • generally audience-appropriate domain-specific vocabulary	
2	• **inconsistent** organizational structure • unclear or somewhat unfocused main idea • inconsistent use of transitions with little variety • formulaic or uneven progression of ideas	• **uneven** support for main idea; **limited** use of sources • weakly integrated, vague, or imprecise evidence from sources • references are vague or absent • weak or uneven elaboration • uneven domain-specific vocabulary	• **adequate** command of spelling, capitalization, punctuation, grammar, and usage • few errors
1	• **little or no** organizational structure • few or no transitions • frequent extraneous ideas; may be formulaic • may lack introduction and/or conclusion • confusing or ambiguous focus; may be very brief	• **minimal** support for main idea; **little or no** use of sources • minimal, absent, incorrect, or irrelevant evidence from sources • references are absent or incorrect • minimal, if any, elaboration • limited or ineffective domain-specific vocabulary	• **partial** command of spelling, capitalization, punctuation, grammar, and usage • some patterns of errors

Teacher Introduction

NARRATIVE PERFORMANCE TASK SCORING RUBRIC

Score	Purpose/Organization	Development/Elaboration	Conventions
4	• **fully sustained** organization; **clear** focus • effective, unified plot • effective development of setting, characters, point of view • transitions clarify relationships between and among ideas • logical sequence of events • effective opening and closing	• **effective** elaboration with details, dialogue, description • clear expression of experiences and events • effective use of relevant source material • effective use of various narrative techniques • effective use of sensory, concrete, and figurative language	
3	• **adequately sustained** organization; **generally maintained** focus • evident plot with loose connections • adequate development of setting, characters, point of view • adequate use of transitional strategies • adequate sequence of events • adequate opening and closing	• **adequate** elaboration with details, dialogue, description • adequate expression of experiences and events • adequate use of source material • adequate use of various narrative techniques • adequate use of sensory, concrete, and figurative language	
2	• **somewhat sustained** organization; **uneven** focus • inconsistent plot with evident flaws • uneven development of setting, characters, point of view • uneven use of transitional strategies, with little variety • weak or uneven sequence of events • weak opening and closing	• **uneven** elaboration with **partial** details, dialogue, description • uneven expression of experiences and events • vague, abrupt, or imprecise use of source material • uneven, inconsistent use of narrative technique • partial or weak use of sensory, concrete, and figurative language	• **adequate** command of spelling, capitalization, punctuation, grammar, and usage • few errors
1	• **basic** organization; **little or no** focus • little or no discernible plot; may just be a series of events • brief or no development of setting, characters, point of view • few or no transitional strategies • little or no organization of event sequence; extraneous ideas • no opening and/or closing	• **minimal** elaboration with **few or no** details, dialogue, description • confusing expression of experiences and events • little or no use of source material • minimal or incorrect use of narrative techniques • little or no use of sensory, concrete, and figurative language	• **partial** command of spelling, capitalization, punctuation, grammar, and usage • some patterns of errors

Teacher Introduction

OPINION PERFORMANCE TASK SCORING RUBRIC

Score	Purpose/Organization	Evidence/Elaboration	Conventions
4	• **effective** organizational structure; **sustained** focus • consistent use of various transitions • logical progression of ideas • effective introduction and conclusion • clearly communicated opinion for purpose, audience, task	• **convincing** support/evidence for main idea; **effective** use of sources; **precise** language • comprehensive evidence from sources is integrated • relevant, specific references • effective elaborative techniques • appropriate domain-specific vocabulary for audience, purpose	
3	• **evident** organizational structure; **adequate** focus • adequate use of transitions • adequate progression of ideas • adequate introduction and conclusion • clear opinion, mostly maintained, though loosely • adequate opinion for purpose, audience, task	• **adequate** support/evidence for main idea; **adequate** use of sources; **general** language • some evidence from sources is integrated • general, imprecise references • adequate elaboration • generally appropriate domain-specific vocabulary for audience, purpose	
2	• **inconsistent** organizational structure; **somewhat sustained** focus • inconsistent use of transitions • uneven progression of ideas • introduction or conclusion, if present, may be weak • somewhat unclear or unfocused opinion	• **uneven** support for main idea; **partial** use of sources; **simple** language • evidence from sources is weakly integrated, vague, or imprecise • vague, unclear references • weak or uneven elaboration • uneven or somewhat ineffective use of domain-specific vocabulary for audience, purpose	• **adequate** command of spelling, capitalization, punctuation, grammar, and usage • few errors
1	• **little or no** organizational structure or focus • few or no transitions • frequent extraneous ideas are evident; may be formulaic • introduction and/or conclusion may be missing • confusing opinion	• **minimal** support for main idea; **little or no** use of sources; **vague** language • source material evidence is minimal, incorrect, or irrelevant • references absent or incorrect • minimal, if any, elaboration • limited or ineffective use of domain-specific vocabulary for audience, purpose	• **partial** command of spelling, capitalization, punctuation, grammar, and usage • some patterns of errors

Teacher Introduction

Evaluating Scores

The goal of each unit assessment is to evaluate student mastery of previously-taught material. The expectation is for students to score 80% or higher on the assessment as a whole. Within this score, the expectation is for students to score 75% or higher on each section of the assessment.

For students who do not meet these benchmarks, assign appropriate lessons from the Tier 2 online PDFs. Refer to the unit assessment pages in the Teacher's Edition of *Reading Wonders* for specific lessons.

The Answer Keys have been constructed to provide the information you need to aid your understanding of student performance, as well as individualized instructional and intervention needs.

This column lists the instructional content from the unit that is assessed in each item.

Question	Answer	Content Focus	CCSS	Complexity

This column lists alignment for each assessment item.

MSR item

This column lists the Depth of Knowledge associated with each item.

Question	Answer	Content Focus	CCSS	Complexity
7	B, E	Main Idea and Key Details	RI.4.2	DOK 2
8	D	Context Clues	L.4.4a	DOK 2
9A	C	Main Idea and Key Details	RI.4.2	DOK 2
9B	B	Main Idea and Key Details/Text Evidence	RI.4.2/RI.4.1	DOK 2

Although text evidence is a key component in all items, it is explicitly called out in EBSR items.

Comprehension: Selected Response 4A, 4B, 5A, 5B, 6A, 6B, 8A, 8B, 10A, 10B, 16A, 16B, 19A, 19B	/14	%
Comprehension: Constructed Response 7, 12, 14, 17, 20, 21	/14	%
Vocabulary 1, 2A, 2B, 3, 9A, 9B, 11, 13, 15, 18	/16	%
English Language Conventions 22–31	/10	%
Total Unit Assessment Score	/54	%

Scoring rows identify items by assessment focus and item type and allow for quick record keeping.

Copyright © McGraw-Hill Education

Teacher Introduction

Teacher Introduction

Evaluating Scores

For PTs, SR items are worth 1 point each. CR items are worth 2 points each.

Use the rubrics to score the full-write.

An anchor paper response can be found in each unit. This top-line response is included to assist with scoring.

The expectation is for students to score 12/15 on the entire task, and 8/10 on the full-write.

Narrative Performance Task					
Question	Answer	CCSS		Complexity	Score
1	B, D	RI.4.1, RI.4.2, RI.4.7, RI.4.8, RI.4.9 W.4.2, W.4.3a-e, W.4.4, W.4.7 L.4.1, L.4.2		DOK 3	/1
2	see below			DOK 3	/2
3	see below			DOK 3	/2
Story	see below			DOK 4	/4 [P/O] /4 [D/E] /2 [C]
Total Score					/15

Read the passage. Then answer the questions.

Helping Others through Business

Do you ever notice things your neighbors need and ways you can make their lives easier? If you do, then you might want to start your own business. Many businesses offer products or services that help others. With help from an adult, you can too! You need to offer services or products that people need or want for your business to succeed. Here are a few ideas for services that you could provide, along with tips to make your business succeed.

Childcare

Many parents are tired after a full day. They might like help caring for their young children. They might be grateful to have someone play with their children while they make dinner. Also, little children love looking at picture books, but they might not be able to read them yet. Consider starting a Parent's Helper service if you like playing with little kids and reading to them.

If you're offering a Parent's Helper service, you might need some training. The Red Cross and other local neighborhood organizations offer courses for young people to learn how to care for young children. If you want your business to succeed, you must know how to take care of children safely.

GO ON →

Garden Care

Pulling weeds and planting flowers takes a lot of work. Some people need help with their yards and gardens. Some neighbors are too busy to rake leaves. If you open a garden care service, you can help your neighbors care for their homes.

Begin by practicing on your own yard, if you have one. You can also practice in a friend's garden. You may be able to use your customers' tools. However, you may need to bring your own tools. Talk to your parents or another adult about borrowing their shovels and rakes. For your first jobs, you may want an adult to come with you in case you need any help.

Pet Care

When people leave town, who takes the dog for a walk? Who changes the kitty litter? Who feeds the goldfish? If you love animals, this is where you come in. Pet care is big business, and every pet owner needs assistance.

Get the word out! Print flyers and business cards with help from an adult. Give your flyers and business cards to people you already know, like family, friends, and close neighbors. The ones who have furry, feathered, or scaly friends will start calling you, and soon you'll have more business than you can handle.

Why not start planning your business today? People are thankful for pet, garden, and childcare services and will come to depend upon you. You can be glad to run a business that helps others, teaches you job skills, and even makes money. Good luck!

GO ON →

1 Read the sentence from the passage.

They might be <u>grateful</u> to have someone play with their children while they make dinner.

If the root word *grat* indicates "pleased or appreciative," what does <u>grateful</u> mean?

(A) beautiful

(B) careful

(C) thankful

(D) thoughtful

2 This question has two parts. First, answer part A. Then, answer part B.

Part A: Read the sentence from the passage.

The Red Cross and other local neighborhood organizations offer <u>courses</u> for young people to learn how to care for young children.

What does the word <u>courses</u> mean in the sentence?

(A) choices

(B) directions

(C) lessons

(D) pathways

Part B: Which sentence **best** supports your answer in part A?

(A) "They might like help caring for their young children."

(B) "Also, little children love looking at picture books, but they might not be able to read them yet."

(C) "If you're offering a Parent's Helper service, you might need some training."

(D) "If you want your business to succeed, you must know how to take care of children safely."

GO ON →

3 Read the sentences from the passage.

Get the word out! Print flyers and business cards with help from an adult. Give your flyers and business cards to people you already know, like family, friends, and close neighbors.

As used in this passage, what does the sentence "Get the word out!" mean? Pick **three** choices.

(A) Talk to everyone you meet.

(B) Look around for pets in the neighborhood.

(C) Let others know about your business.

(D) Ask for help if you need it.

(E) Make phone calls to family and friends.

(F) Write down your business plans and goals.

4 This question has two parts. First, answer part A. Then, answer part B.

Part A: What do the subheadings in the passage help the reader understand?

(A) the main types of businesses young people could start

(B) the three ways to market a business in the neighborhood

(C) the most important keys to creating a successful business

(D) the usual kinds of businesses that kids start without equipment

Part B: Which sentence from the passage **best** supports your answer in part A?

(A) "Here are a few ideas for services that you could provide, along with tips to make your business succeed."

(B) "Consider starting a Parent's Helper service if you like playing with little kids and reading to them."

(C) "Print flyers and business cards with help from an adult."

(D) "People are thankful for pet, garden, and childcare services and will come to depend upon you."

GO ON →

5 The following question has two parts. First, answer part A. Then, answer part B.

Part A: Which sentence **best** states the main idea of the passage?

(A) Many people living nearby are struggling at home.

(B) Doing yard work is a great way to start a small business.

(C) Local groups often help young people learn important skills.

(D) Starting a successful business often means finding a way to help others.

Part B: Which sentence from the passage **best** supports your answer in part A?

(A) "Do you ever notice things your neighbors need and ways you can make their lives easier?"

(B) "You need to offer services or products that people need or want for your business to succeed."

(C) "The Red Cross and other local neighborhood organizations offer courses for young people to learn how to care for young children."

(D) "Pulling weeds and planting flowers takes a lot of work."

GO ON →

6 The following question has two parts. First, answer part A. Then, answer part B.

Part A: Which sentence is the **best** summary of the ideas in the last two paragraphs of the passage?

(A) Waiting until a certain age to start a business is a mistake.

(B) Starting a business often requires the purchase of different tools.

(C) Advertising personal services is the key to creating a successful business.

(D) Having a business at a young age can benefit a young person in many ways.

Part B: Which sentence from the passage **best** supports your answer in part A?

(A) "Print flyers and business cards with help from an adult."

(B) "Give your flyers and business cards to people you already know, like family, friends, and close neighbors."

(C) "People are thankful for pet, garden, and childcare services and will come to depend upon you."

(D) "You can be glad to run a business that helps others, teaches you job skills, and even makes money."

7 Based on what you read in "Helping Others through Business," what are the keys to a successful business? Support your answer with at least **two** details from the passage.

_____

_____

_____

_____

_____

_____

GO ON →

Read the passage. Then answer the questions.

A Mountain Dream

For years, Lisa Ricci had worked in her family's New York City bakery. She had enjoyed learning about the baking business. She loved seeing how many customers came back week after week for more, and she often handed children free sugar cookies just to see the smiles on their faces.

But Lisa was ready for an adventure. She liked New York, but the tall buildings couldn't hide the fact that the city was flat. Lisa yearned for a future that wasn't laid out and stretched thin before her like rolled dough. Lisa dreamed of the Rocky Mountains. Her friend Cindy Hooper owned a bed and breakfast inn near Loveland, Colorado. Cindy invited Lisa to come work with her. Lisa imagined exploring the snow-capped peaks of the Rockies. She wanted to picnic in valleys filled with golden Aspen trees, dip her toes in cool, clear rivers, and watch elk feed at dusk.

In late summer, Lisa moved to Loveland and she and Cindy agreed on a work schedule. Lisa would work Wednesday through Sunday, which sounded perfect. On her days off, she would go hiking in the Rockies. Lisa was so excited! She could hardly believe her luck.

One week into her new job, the luck that brought her to Colorado seemed to change. While changing a light bulb, Cindy fell from a stepladder and broke her leg. Cindy's leg would be a cast for three months. Lisa wouldn't think of leaving her dear friend high and dry, so she toiled around the clock.

Lisa never complained. Months went by, and Lisa hadn't gone to the mountains once. There was a chill in the air and soon winter would arrive. Lisa wouldn't have another chance to hike until spring. She was so close to the Rocky Mountains, and yet she couldn't seem to reach them.

GO ON →

Three months passed. Cindy's leg healed, and her cast came off. Finally, Lisa felt she could go off and explore. She joined Happy Trails Hiking Club. The club had organized a day hike that Monday in Estes Park. All Lisa had to do was walk three blocks to the corner and board a bus by 10 a.m. That would work just fine. Lisa told Cindy she would serve breakfast on Monday, even though it was her day off. Breakfast always ended at 9:30, so she would still have time to catch the bus.

Lisa cleaned up the last of the breakfast dishes and wiped down the tables. At 9:45, she buttoned up her coat, filled her water bottle and laced up her hiking boots. Just as she was about to leave, two guests came downstairs. "Are we too late for breakfast?" they asked.

Cindy returned at 10:30 to find Lisa still there, cleaning up again. "You missed your bus!" she exclaimed, loud enough for the two guests to hear her. "It's no big deal," Lisa insisted. "Besides," Lisa said, pointing at snow flurries out the window, "it's not a great day to hike anyway." But after Cindy explained to the guests all that Lisa had done for her, they made her an offer. "We're going skiing today. We have an extra ticket for going skiing. Would you like to come with us?"

When Lisa got in the car, Cindy handed her a sealed envelope through the window. Halfway into the mountains, Lisa remembered to open it. Inside were a note and enough money for Lisa to buy a season pass and also pay for her ski and boot rentals. "Your mountain dream is finally coming true," said the note. "Did you know that my dream of having a great friend came true as well?"

GO ON →

8 The following question has two parts. First, answer part A. Then, answer part B.

Part A: Which statement **best** explains why Lisa moves to Colorado?

(A) Lisa wants to meet different people.

(B) Lisa has a friend who has an inn in Colorado.

(C) Lisa wants to climb the mountains in Colorado.

(D) Lisa has a friend who needs her help to run her business.

Part B: Which sentence from the passage **best** supports your answer in part A?

(A) "For years, Lisa Ricci had worked in her family's New York City bakery."

(B) "Lisa yearned for a future that wasn't laid out and stretched thin before her like rolled dough."

(C) "Her friend Cindy Hooper owned a bed and breakfast inn near Loveland, Colorado."

(D) "Cindy's leg would be in a cast for three months."

GO ON →

9 The following question has two parts. First, answer part A. Then, answer part B.

Part A: Read the sentence from the passage.

One week into her new job, the <u>luck</u> that brought her to Colorado seemed to change.

Which word means the almost the same as <u>luck</u> as it is used in the sentence?

(A) effort

(B) fortune

(C) opportunity

(D) surprise

Part B: Which sentence from the passage supports your answer in part A?

(A) "Lisa would work Wednesday through Sunday, which sounded perfect."

(B) "On her days off, she would go hiking in the Rockies."

(C) "Lisa wouldn't think of leaving her dear friend high and dry, so she toiled around the clock."

(D) "Just as she was about to leave, two guests came downstairs."

GO ON →

10 The following question has two parts. First, answer part A. Then, answer part B.

Part A: What stops Lisa from exploring the Rocky Mountains sooner?

(A) She cares about her friend.

(B) She needs to earn more money.

(C) She wants to find others to hike with.

(D) She is confused about how to get there.

Part B: Which sentence from the passage supports your answer in part A?

(A) "She was so close to the Rocky Mountains, and yet she couldn't seem to reach them."

(B) "She joined Happy Trails Hiking Club."

(C) "Cindy returned to find Lisa still there, cleaning up again."

(D) "Inside were a note and enough money for Lisa to buy a season pass and also pay for her ski and boot rentals."

GO ON →

11 Read the sentence from the passage.

Lisa wouldn't think of leaving her dear friend <u>high and dry</u>, so she <u>toiled around the clock</u>.

Draw a line to match each idiom with one phrase from the list that **most closely** matches it.

high and dry   worked every single day with few breaks

                               was on time for every shift she was assigned

toiled around   alone and frightened
the clock

                               put out of sight for a while

                               left alone without any help

12 Find **three** events that happened after Cindy's cast came off. Write a number from 1-3 next to these three events to show the order in which they occurred.

_____ Lisa imagined hiking in the Rocky Mountains.

_____ Lisa joined the Happy Trails Hiking Club.

_____ Lisa was given money to buy a season pass and ski and boot rentals.

_____ Lisa moved to Loveland to help in the bed and breakfast inn.

_____ Lisa made plans to go on a day hike to Estes Park.

_____ Lisa handed out sugar cookies to some of her favorite customers.

GO ON →

13 Read the sentence from the passage.

All Lisa had to do was walk three blocks to the corner and <u>board</u> a bus by 10 a.m.

Which sentence uses the same meaning of the word <u>board</u> as in the sentence from the passage?

(A) She pays for room and board.

(B) He has to board the plane early.

(C) They cut the board into many pieces.

(D) We will board up the broken window.

14 Explain what the main problem is in "A Mountain Dream" and how it is solved. Use **two** details from the passage to support your answer.

_____

_____

_____

_____

_____

_____

GO ON →

Read the passages. Then answer the questions.

Communicating Coast to Coast

In 1850, the United States Congress passed a bill making California the thirty-first state. It took nine weeks for the news to reach California. Today, news like that would zoom across the country in an instant.

Traveling to the West

Gold was discovered in California in 1848. This caused many Americans to head to the West Coast in search of fortunes. It was known as the "gold rush," but no one got there quickly. The cheapest way to travel west was by covered wagon. It was also the slowest. A wagon trip from St. Louis, Missouri, took about six months.

Some people traveled by sea. Ships sailed around South America. The trip from New York City to San Francisco was more than 16,000 miles. One ship made the trip in 89 days in 1851, but people wanted faster ways to travel. More importantly, they wanted faster ways to send information.

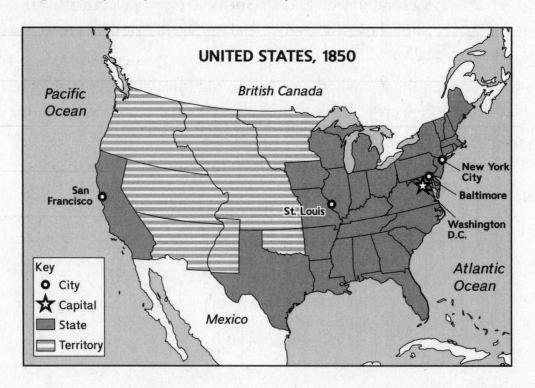

GO ON →

Carrying the Mail

In 1858, stagecoaches began carrying mail. Letters traveled from St. Louis to San Francisco in just 25 days. Soon the mail traveled even faster when carried on horseback. The Pony Express was a series of stations across the West. Riders on horseback carried a pouch of mail from one station to the next. The first rider handed the mail pouch to the next rider, who rode off at great speed. At the next station, the pouch was handed off again, and so on until it reached the final station.

The Pony Express helped information travel more quickly. However, a revolutionary change in the way messages traveled was already taking place. A man named Samuel Morse was leading the way.

Connecting East and West

Morse overheard people discussing whether it would be possible to send messages along a wire. The idea excited him. He knew electricity traveled along a wire in an instant. Imagine sending messages that way!

His inventive mind got right to work. Morse soon had a working model of a telegraph. This machine started and stopped the flow of electricity. This created long and short bursts of energy that represented letters and numbers. This alphabet is called Morse code.

Morse dreamed of the day when messages could travel thousands of miles in minutes. But there were still many problems to solve. It would not be easy to string telegraph wires across the nation. Morse needed a lot of money to get it done. He decided to ask the United States government for help.

GO ON →

When Morse first presented his idea to Congress, they thought his idea seemed impossible. Eventually, Congress gave Morse enough money to get started. He demonstrated how the telegraph worked by sending a message from Baltimore, Maryland, to Washington, D.C. It worked! Those who had made fun of him were convinced. They regretted having ridiculed him.

Connecting the nation from coast to coast by telegraph was a big job. Finally, in 1861, wires from the East joined wires from the West and the transcontinental telegraph was complete! As soon as the telegraph reached completely across the continent, news traveled at lightning speed. This led to the end of the Pony Express because even the fastest horses were no match for the telegraph.

Into the Future

Most telegraph messages were short. Because telegraph offices were not located in every town, many people still sent family news through the mail. Still, the telegraph paved the way for today's high-speed world of telephones, cell phones, text messages, television, radio, and the Internet.

GO ON →

Theodore Judah and the Road West

During the 1850s, many people believed that a railroad could not be built across the United States. They claimed the mountains and deserts of the West could not be crossed. Theodore Judah, however, was sure the job could be done.

Judah was an American railroad engineer who dreamed of the first transcontinental railroad. Judah studied engineering in college. After working on several railroads in the Northeast, he was hired to work for a railroad in California.

He continued to focus on his dream of connecting the East and West. He was sometimes called "Crazy Judah" because of this dream. But he was determined to reach his goal. As the chief engineer of the Central Pacific Railroad, he began laying tracks eastward from California. Tracks for the Union Pacific Railroad were being laid from the East at the same time. The plan was to join the tracks somewhere in the middle of the country. This would form the transcontinental railroad.

The Difficult Path Ahead

Building the Central Pacific Railroad was a challenge. Lying directly in the railroad's path were the Sierra Nevada Mountains. These mountains had cliffs sharp as knives that dropped without warning into steep canyons. If Judah and his crew were going to succeed, they had to figure out how to lay tracks through this rugged territory. Workers were lowered over cliffs in baskets. They used hammers to carve paths into the sides of the mountains. Then these paths were widened enough to lay railroad tracks. It was slow work.

Judah and his crew faced many obstacles. During the first winter, the wind piled snow 50 feet high. Wooden snow sheds were built to protect the workers and the tracks. Even with this protection, there were problems. As a result of the cold, workers suffered from frostbite. Judah often ordered these workers to be sent back to California for treatment.

The slowest work was digging Summit Tunnel. Day and night, hammers and chisels bit into the rock. Even though the men worked constantly, they only removed about two inches of rock a day. It was the most expensive quarter-mile of railroad track in history.

GO ON →

Finally, their hard work paid off. Judah and his men had crossed the Sierra Nevada! Unfortunately they faced a new challenge. They had to work in the desert heat of the Great Basin.

Even with all these difficulties, the Central Pacific Railroad joined the Union Pacific Railroad in 1869. At Promontory, Utah, a crowd of people were

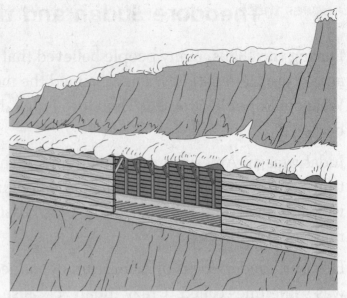

Snow sheds allowed work to continue throughout the winter.

thrilled to see a golden spike driven into the tracks to mark the special occasion. Unfortunately, Theodore Judah died before the railroad was completed, but he and many other brave people proved it could be done.

GO ON →

Answer these questions about "Communicating Coast to Coast."

15 Read the sentences from the passage.

Those who had made fun of him were convinced. They <u>regretted</u> having ridiculed him.

Which words from the sentences help to explain what <u>ridiculed</u> means?

Ⓐ Those who had

Ⓑ made fun of

Ⓒ were convinced

Ⓓ They regretted

16 The following question has two parts. First, answer part A. Then, answer part B.

Part A: What is the main idea of the passage?

Ⓐ Many people participated in the gold rush.

Ⓑ Methods of communication improved after 1850.

Ⓒ It took a long time for people to travel around in 1850.

Ⓓ The telegraph replaced other means of communication.

Part B: Which sentence from the passage **best** supports your answer in part A?

Ⓐ "This caused many Americans to head to the West Coast in search of fortunes."

Ⓑ "The trip from New York City to San Francisco was more than 16,000 miles."

Ⓒ "Finally, in 1861, wires from the East joined wires from the West and the transcontinental telegraph was complete!"

Ⓓ "This led to the end of the Pony Express because even the fastest horses were no match for the telegraph."

GO ON →

17 What role did Congress play in the development of the telegraph? Use **two** details from the passage to support your answer.

_____

_____

_____

_____

_____

GO ON →

Name: _____ Date: _____

Answer these questions about "Theodore Judah and the Road West."

18 Read the sentence from the passage.

These mountains had cliffs sharp as knives that dropped without warning into <u>steep</u> canyons.

Which sentence uses the same meaning of the word <u>steep</u> as in the sentence from the passage?

Ⓐ The price of soap had a steep increase.

Ⓑ They steep the tea in water for three minutes.

Ⓒ They have a class that will steep them in history.

Ⓓ The trail to the cabin has a steep edge on one side.

19 What was **one** difficulty that Judah and the workers had after crossing the Sierra Nevada Mountains?

Ⓐ Workers were constantly chipping at the rock to dig the tunnel.

Ⓑ There were workers laying tracks from the East at the same time.

Ⓒ The heat in the Great Basin desert made it difficult for the workers.

Ⓓ Workers had to be sent in baskets over the cliffs to cross the mountains.

GO ON →

20 What is the overall structure of the passage? Use **two** details from the passage to support your answer.

_____

_____

_____

_____

_____

_____

Now answer this question about "Communicating Coast to Coast" and "Theodore Judah and the Road West."

21 In both "Communicating Coast to Coast" and "Theodore Judah and the Road West," the authors describe how Morse and Judah had ideas that changed American society. How did their actions improve the lives of others? Support your answer with clear evidence from both passages.

_____

_____

_____

_____

_____

_____

_____

_____

_____

_____

_____

_____

_____

_____

GO ON →

The passage below needs revision. Read the passage. Then answer the questions.

(1) Kayla was reading a story to two squirmy twins their names were Jerome and Ella. (2) The story was about a little monkey named Chester. (3) Always getting into trouble.

(4) Jerome and Ella started to giggle. (5) The story was so funny. (6) Kayla just kept on reading. (7) Jerome giggled and squirmed so much that he fell off the bed. (8) Ella gasped, and Kayla stopped reading.

(9) Luckily, the pillows that were usually on the bed were on the floor. (10) After Jerome got over his surprise, he said, "That was fun!" (11) Everybody laughed. (12) He climbed back up on the bed and rolled off onto the pillows again.

(13) "You are a lot like Chester," said Kayla.

(14) "I'm a monkey!" shouted Jerome. (15) "Monkeys like bananas so do I."

(16) They all went to the kitchen, they found a bunch of bananas in a bowl. (17) "You need to calm down before you can eat," said Kayla. (18) Jerome did not agree. (19) He started to grab a banana Kayla got there first. (20) She held the bowl high in the air. (21) "Close your eyes and count slowly to ten." (22) Jerome calmed down. (23) Ate half a banana before bed.

GO ON →

22 Which of these is a run-on sentence?

Ⓐ Sentence 1

Ⓑ Sentence 2

Ⓒ Sentence 3

Ⓓ Sentence 7

23 What is the subject of sentence 2?

Ⓐ Chester

Ⓑ the story

Ⓒ was

Ⓓ a little monkey

24 What is the **best** way to write sentence 3 as a complete sentence?

Ⓐ Fun to be always getting into trouble.

Ⓑ Because Chester was always getting into trouble.

Ⓒ Chester was always getting into trouble.

Ⓓ Enjoying himself always getting into trouble.

GO ON →

25 Which is the **best** way to combine sentences 4 and 5?

(A) Jerome and Ella started to giggle, or the story was so funny.

(B) Jerome and Ella started to giggle, and the story was so funny.

(C) Jerome and Ella started to giggle why the story was so funny.

(D) Jerome and Ella started to giggle because the story was so funny.

26 Which sentence is a compound sentence?

(A) Sentence 6

(B) Sentence 7

(C) Sentence 8

(D) Sentence 9

27 Which sentence contains a subordinate clause?

(A) Sentence 8

(B) Sentence 10

(C) Sentence 11

(D) Sentence 18

GO ON →

28 Which of these is a run-on sentence?

Ⓐ Sentence 7

Ⓑ Sentence 9

Ⓒ Sentence 12

Ⓓ Sentence 19

29 How can sentence 15 **best** be written as a compound sentence?

Ⓐ "Monkeys like bananas, and so do I."

Ⓑ "Monkeys like bananas because I do."

Ⓒ "Monkeys like bananas before I do."

Ⓓ "Monkeys like bananas, or so do I."

30 What is the **best** way to write sentence 16 as a complex sentence?

Ⓐ They all went to the kitchen, found a bunch of bananas in a bowl.

Ⓑ They all went to the kitchen, but they found a bunch of bananas in a bowl.

Ⓒ They all went to the kitchen, also found a bunch of bananas in a bowl.

Ⓓ They all went to the kitchen, where they found a bunch of bananas in a bowl.

GO ON →

31 Which of these is a sentence fragment because it **does not** have a subject?

Ⓐ Sentence 18

Ⓑ Sentence 20

Ⓒ Sentence 22

Ⓓ Sentence 23

Narrative Performance Task

Task:

Your class is learning about how challenges bring out the best in people. Each student must write a story to include in a class book. Before your teacher assigns the story, you do some research and find two articles that provide information about famous people who have overcome challenges.

After you have looked at these sources, you will answer some questions about them. Briefly scan the sources and the three questions that follow. Then, go back and read the sources carefully to gain the information you will need to answer the questions and complete your research.

In Part 2, you will write a story using the information you have read.

Directions for Part 1

You will now look at two sources. You can look at either of the sources as often as you like.

Research Questions:

After looking at the sources, use the rest of the time in Part 1 to answer three questions about them. Your answers to these questions will be scored. Also, your answers will help you think about the information you have read, which should help you write your story. You may refer to the sources when you think it would be helpful. You may also look at your notes.

GO ON →

Source #1: A Show of Courage

The Boy Scouts had been planning the celebration for weeks. Now, the day was here. They were gathered on New York's Bear Mountain for the summer jamboree! The scouts were even getting a visit from Franklin Delano Roosevelt, known as FDR, who was running for vice president of the United States.

As FDR made his rounds at the gathering that day, he shook hands with the scouts and enjoyed a special dinner with them. It was most likely during this visit that a virus would enter his body and change the politician's life forever.

The trip to nearby Campobello Island was supposed to be a vacation. FDR had spent years attending college, getting married and starting a family, and running for office. He was ready to relax. He brought three of his children with him to the family's summer cottage. On that August day, they went sailing, swimming, and hiking. By the time FDR went to bed that evening, he was quite tired. When he awoke in the morning, he was more than tired—he was extremely ill. By the end of the day, pain had spread to his neck and back. He could not move either of his legs.

At first the doctors were puzzled. Finally, FDR went to a specialist who told the 39-year-old FDR that he had polio. It was the worst news possible. Roosevelt was running for office! He had important plans! Rather than give up, Roosevelt decided he was not going to let this disease stop him.

FDR and his family worked hard to help him get better. He exercised and soaked in warm mineral springs to improve his muscles. He refused to sit in his wheelchair very often. Instead, he wore heavy braces on his legs to help him walk. Although there was some improvement, Roosevelt never was able to walk very far.

This might have been enough to defeat many people, but it only strengthened FDR. He went on to become one of the country's most beloved presidents. He was the only president ever elected to four terms in a row. He helped the country through some of its most difficult challenges, including the Great Depression of the 1930s and World War II in the 1940s.

Roosevelt also changed countless lives in another way. Each year, on his birthday, a dance was held to raise money for polio research. FDR also

GO ON →

started a program called the March of Dimes. It brought in millions of dollars from people all over the country. The money was used to find a cure for the disease. Although a vaccine was not found until ten years after FDR's death, it was his struggle—and his courage—that made a cure possible.

Source #2: A Different Way of Thinking

Today, Temple Grandin is a scientist, author, and professor. She has given lectures to countless people. She has helped make sure that animals are treated kindly. She has also won many awards for her successes. All of this would have been impossible for her family, doctor, and even Grandin herself, to imagine when she was a child.

In 1949, Grandin's mother took her daughter to a doctor. She wanted to find out why her two-year-old was not talking yet. Why didn't she want to be touched? Why did she spend hours watching spinning plates or humming to herself? What was the reason for her screaming temper tantrums? The doctors told Grandin's mother that Temple was autistic. Little was known about autism at that time. The doctors did not believe the young child would ever speak or be able to go to school.

Grandin's mother disagreed. She began reading to her daughter every day. She took her to speech therapy. By age four, Grandin was talking. She went to school, but it was not easy for her. There was so much to see, hear, smell, and touch that Grandin sometimes had panic attacks. Her life changed when she began spending summers at her aunt's cattle ranch. She spent a great deal of time watching the cows. The ranchers put the animals in a squeeze chute to hold them still and calm them while they were getting vaccinated. Grandin was fascinated. She built her own squeeze chute in her bedroom. She crawled into it whenever she felt the need to be held tight and calmed. Today, an updated version of that chute is used in schools and treatment centers for autistic children.

While at the ranch, Grandin also realized something else important. She felt connected to the cattle. It was as if she could see and feel what they were experiencing. She did not think in words like most people. Instead, she thought in pictures. Seeing how the cattle were treated at the ranch

GO ON →

gave her many ideas of how farms and ranches could change their methods. Just a few changes would make taking care of cattle easier for the owners, and for the animals. Grandin went to college and earned several degrees in animal science. She designed new and different kinds of livestock equipment.

At first, ranchers did not listen to Grandin. They were not used to a woman, especially an autistic woman, telling them they had to make changes. It did not take long, however, before they realized how much better her designs worked for cattle. In 1975, Grandin started her own company.

Since then, Grandin has written several books about autism and a movie has been made about her life. She gives talks to people all over the world and answers parents' questions about their autistic children. She reminds them that just because some people's brains see the world differently, they can still invent, create, and make the planet a better place for everyone.

GO ON →

1 How do paragraphs 1 through 3 add to Source #1? Pick **all** choices that answer the question correctly.

(A) They describe the damaging effects of the polio virus.

(B) They suggest how FDR may have caught the polio virus.

(C) They explain how germs can spread easily among people.

(D) They show that the politician will never be the same again.

(E) They explain the importance of FDR at that point in history.

(F) They show that little medical treatment was available for polio.

(G) They explain why the Boy Scouts were excited about the celebration.

2 The sources explain the physical challenges that FDR and Temple Grandin faced. Explain why this information is important to understanding each person's success. Use **one** example from Source #1 and **one** example from Source #2 to support your explanation. For each example, include the source title and number.

_____

_____

_____

_____

_____

GO ON →

3 Source #1 and Source #2 discuss how others helped FDR and Temple Grandin deal with their physical challenges. Explain what the sources say about helping others. Use **one** detail from Source #1 and **one** detail from Source #2 to support your explanation. For each detail, include the source title or number.

_____

_____

_____

_____

_____

GO ON →

Directions for Part 2

You will now look at your sources, take notes, and plan, draft, revise, and edit your article. First, read your assignment and the information about how your informational article will be scored. Then begin your work.

Your Assignment:

A visitor comes to your class and describes how she trains companion dogs to help people who have physical challenges. After she is done, your teacher assigns you to write a story about a companion dog for either FDR or Temple Grandin. Imagine that the dog is lying quietly on the rug when there is a knock on the door. In your story, describe how the dog helps FDR or Grandin with his or her physical challenges. The story should be several paragraphs long.

Writers often do research to add realistic details to the setting, characters, and plot in their stories. When writing your story, find ways to use information and details from the sources to improve your story and help you develop your characters, the setting, and the plot. Use details, dialogue, and description where appropriate.

REMEMBER: A well-written story

• has a clear plot and clear sequence of events

• is well-organized and has a point of view

• uses details from more than one source to support your story

• uses clear language

• follows rules of writing (spelling, punctuation, and grammar usage)

Now begin work on your story. Manage your time carefully so that you can plan, write, revise, and edit the final draft of your story. Write your response on a separate sheet of paper.

Question	Correct Answer	Content Focus	CCSS	Complexity
1	C	Suffixes: *-ful*	L.4.4b	DOK 1
2A	C	Context Clues: Multiple-Meaning Words	L.4.4a	DOK 2
2B	C	Context Clues: Multiple-Meaning Words/ Text Evidence	L.4.4a/ RI.4.1	DOK 2
3	A, C, E	Context Clues: Definitions and Restatements	L.4.4a	DOK 2
4A	A	Text Features: Heads and Subheads	RI.4.7	DOK 2
4B	D	Text Features: Heads and Subheads/ Text Evidence	RI.4.7/ RI.4.1	DOK 2
5A	D	Main Idea and Key Details	RI.4.2	DOK 2
5B	B	Main Idea and Key Details/Text Evidence	RI.4.2/ RI.4.1	DOK 2
6A	D	Main Idea and Key Details	RI.4.2	DOK 2
6B	D	Main Idea and Key Details/Text Evidence	RI.4.2/ RI.4.1	DOK 2
7	see below	Text Structure: Cause and Effect/ Text Evidence	RI.4.5/ RI.4.1	DOK 3
8A	C	Character, Setting, Plot: Sequence	RL.4.3	DOK 2
8B	B	Character, Setting, Plot: Sequence/ Text Evidence	RL.4.3/ RL.4.1	DOK 2
9A	B	Context Clues: Synonyms	L.4.5c	DOK 2
9B	C	Context Clues: Synonyms/Text Evidence	L.4.5c/ RL.4.1	DOK 2
10A	A	Character, Setting, Plot: Problem and Solution	RL.4.3	DOK 2
10B	C	Character, Setting, Plot: Problem and Solution/Text Evidence	RL.4.3/ RL.4.1	DOK 2
11	see below	Figurative Language: Idioms	L.4.5b	DOK 2
12	see below	Character, Setting, Plot: Sequence	RL.4.3	DOK 1
13	B	Context Clues: Multiple-Meaning Words	L.4.4a	DOK 2
14	see below	Character, Setting, Plot: Problem and Solution	RL.4.3	DOK 3
15	B	Context Clues: Definitions and Restatements	L.4.4a	DOK 1
16A	B	Main Idea and Key Details	RI.4.2	DOK 2
16B	C	Main Idea and Key Details/Text Evidence	RI.4.2/ RI.4.1	DOK 2
17	see below	Text Structure: Cause and Effect	RI.4.5	DOK 3
18	D	Context Clues: Multiple- Meaning Words	L.4.4a	DOK 2

Question	Correct Answer	Content Focus	CCSS	Complexity
19	C	Main Idea and Key Details	RI.4.2	DOK 2
20	see below	Text Structure: Cause and Effect	RI.4.5	DOK 3
21	see below	Compare Across Texts	W.4.9b	DOK 4
22	A	Run-on Sentences	L.4.1f	DOK 1
23	B	Subjects and Predicates	L.4.1f	DOK 1
24	C	Sentences	L.4.3a	DOK 1
25	D	Clauses and Complex Sentences	L.4.1f	DOK 1
26	C	Compound Sentences	L.4.2c	DOK 1
27	B	Clauses and Complex Sentences	L.4.2c	DOK 1
28	D	Run-on Sentences	L.4.1f	DOK 1
29	A	Compound Sentences	L.4.1f	DOK 1
30	D	Clauses and Complex Sentences	L.4.1f	DOK 1
31	D	Subjects and Predicates	L.4.1f	DOK 1

Comprehension: Selected Response 4A, 4B, 5A, 5B, 6A, 6B, 8A, 8B, 10A, 10B, 16A, 16B, 19	/14	%
Comprehension: Constructed Response 7, 12, 14, 17, 20, 21	/14	%
Vocabulary 1, 2A, 2B, 3, 9A, 9B, 11, 13, 15, 18	/16	%
English Language Conventions 22-31	/10	%
Total Unit Assessment Score	/54	%

7 **2-point response:** The main keys to a successful business are offering products or services that help others. It is important to look around you and find what other people may need. Some of the needs that people have are help with kids, pets, and yard work.

14 **2-point response:** The problem is that Lisa is working so hard for her friend Cindy that she does not get the chance to go to the mountains, which is the reason she moved to Colorado in the first place. The problem is finally solved when Cindy sees how much Lisa is giving up. She arranges for Lisa to go skiing and gives her all the money she needs to get a pass and rent her ski equipment.

11 Students should draw lines to match the following:
 • high and dry: left alone without any help
 • toiled around the clock: worked every single day with few breaks

12 Students should number the following three events as shown:

1. Lisa joined the Happy Trails Hiking Club.

2. Lisa made plans to go on a day hike to Estes Park.

3. Lisa was given money to buy a season pass and ski and boot rentals.

17 **2-point response:** Morse had a very good idea when he thought of the telegraph, but making the idea actually happen was going to take a lot of money. By deciding to believe that his idea of the telegraph could actually work and by providing the money to run the wires across the country, Congress made it possible for Morse's invention to be put into place.

20 **2-point response:** Judah was a good candidate to work for the transcontinental railroad not just because he studied engineering in college but also because he really believed that the United States could be connected by the railroads. Most people at the time believed this could not be done, but Judah helped the crews to overcome great obstacles to help connect the two sides of the country.

21 **4-point response:** Both Morse and Judah had ideas that made it possible for the many parts of the country to be connected to each other. Morse's invention of the telegraph made it possible for information to be sent across the entire country in no time at all. This was a very big change, since until then, people had to wait for the Pony Express to bring messages. The telegraph is not a way we think of sending information now, but the telegraph was an important first step toward the many ways we can communicate now.

Judah's dream of connecting the country by railway made it possible for people to quickly and safely travel from one side of the United States to the other. Before the railroad lines were in place, people who wanted to go from the East Coast to the West Coast had to decide between taking a wagon trip or sailing around South America. Neither of those methods were safe or quick. By working to help make sure that the tracks were laid so that trains could travel from coast to coast, Judah helped to make it possible to connect the different parts of the United States. The deserts and the mountains in the West were very challenging to lay tracks through, but by being determined to make it happen, Judah made travel across the United States much easier.

Answer Key

Narrative Performance Task				
Question	Answer	CCSS	Complexity	Score
1	B, D, E	RI.4.1, RI.4.2, RI.4.8, RI.4.9 W.4.3a-e, W.4.4, W.4.7 L.4.1, L.4.2	DOK 3	/1
2	see below		DOK 3	/2
3	see below		DOK 3	/2
Narrative Story	see below		DOK 4	/4 [P/O] /4 [D/E] /2 [C]
Total Score				/15

2 **2-point response:** The information about the physical challenges that Roosevelt and Grandin faced helps the reader understand how impressive it is that Roosevelt and Grandin achieved so much success. Source #1 tells how, despite needing heavy braces on his legs to walk and being unable to walk far, Roosevelt was elected to four terms as U.S. President and helped the country through the Great Depression and World War II. Source #2 tells how, despite her trouble learning to talk and going to school, Grandin earned several degrees and now gives talks about autism to people around the world.

3 **2-point response:** The descriptions of how other people helped Roosevelt and Grandin deal with their physical challenges show that people can make the world a better place by trying to help people. Source #1 says that Roosevelt and his family worked hard to help him get better. His doctors figured out what was wrong with him, and people all over the country donated money to try to find a cure, and finally a vaccine was found. Source #2 tells how Grandin's mother read to her every day and took her to speech therapy to teach her to talk. If her mother had accepted what the doctors said and given up trying to teach her to talk, Grandin might never have been able to go to school and then to write books.

10-point anchor paper: As I lay on the warm rug, listening lazily to the fire crackling in the fireplace, I enjoyed the warmth that filled the room. I was just about to drift off to sleep when Prez rolled into the room. I called him Prez, but just about everyone else, except his family, called him Mr. President. His full name was Franklin Delano Roosevelt, and he was my master and the President of the United States.

I am a service dog, and I came to live with him after he became sick with polio. It is a terrible illness that has no cure. I spent a long time being trained especially for him. It was my job to help him, in any way that I could. I brought him things, alerted him to dangerous situations, or just sat by him and let him pet my long, golden fur. He seemed to enjoy the petting most of all. I did too.

Quickly, I jumped up to greet him. I stood in front of him, wagging my tail to let him know how happy I was to see him.

"Sammy," he asked me, "are you enjoying the warmth of that fire on this cold December day?" He rolled closer to feel the warmth himself.

Knowing the routine, I grabbed the newspaper from the table and brought it to him. After I set it in his lap, I licked his hand, and nudged my nose under it, wanting a good pet.

"You are such a good dog, Sammy. Always right there when I need you." Rubbing the backs of my ears in appreciation, Prez looked intently at the opened newspaper. He scanned the dark shapes on the pages. I never quite understood why he did this, but he seemed to think it was important. He often became angered by whatever he saw.

After a long pause, he sighed. "Oh, why don't they listen? Things will never get better without everyone helping!"

Dropping the paper in his lap, he looked at me seriously. "Sammy, go get Mrs. Roosevelt."

Immediately I sprinted out the door, and down the hall to find Mrs. Roosevelt. When I found her, she was just finishing with breakfast. Excited to complete my job, I bounded into the room and gave a short bark to get her attention.

"Sammy?" she asked. But, then, understanding why I was there, she replied, "I am coming." She hurried down the hall to Prez's office.

"Is everything all right, dear?" she asked, even before fully entering the room.

"Oh, yes," he answered, sounding frustrated. "I didn't mean to alarm you. I just need to go meet with my staff. I think I might have an idea that will help our troops fighting in the war. Sammy, grab my case and follow me! We are going to work!"

Grabbing his case, I followed him. I knew that I would need to be right by his side, helping him, all day. I would help him by holding open doors, bringing him important files, and even bringing him the case that held the braces that he sometimes wore on his legs. I was his companion dog, and I was there to help him however I could.

Read the poem. Then answer the questions.

Acrobats of the Ocean

The darkened sky recedes at dawn.
Black ocean turns to blue.
A distant sound breaks through the air
As dolphins come into view.

Like birds on air they rise and jump,
Light dancing off their skin.
They squeak and chatter through the waves.
They leap, they chase, they spin.

They swim as fast as lightning
And protect others in their pod.
Jumping high like shooting stars,
They leave observers awed.

These ballet dancers of the sea
Slap tails, butt heads, and play.
Their curved mouths always smiling,
They look and swim away.

I'd like to be a dolphin,
Taking care of those I love
While dancing in the ocean air,
Sun shining warm above.

GO ON →

1 Read the lines from the poem.

The darkened sky <u>recedes</u> at dawn.
Black ocean turns to blue.

Draw lines to match **two** words that mean **nearly** the opposite
of <u>recedes</u>.

recedes   advances

recedes   approaches

                                           lessens

                                           hides

                                           remains

GO ON →

2 The following question has two parts. First, answer part A. Then, answer part B.

Part A: Which sentence **best** states the theme of the poem?

(A) Dolphins are very happy creatures.

(B) Dolphins are extremely fast.

(C) Dolphins move much like birds do.

(D) Dolphins are the performers of the sea.

Part B: Which line from the poem **best** supports your answer in Part A?

(A) Like birds on air they rise and jump,

(B) They swim as fast as lightning

(C) They leave observers awed.

(D) Their curved mouths always smiling,

3 Explain how the speaker's comparisons of dolphins to other things help the reader understand the speaker's point of view. Use **two** details from the poem to support your answer.

_____

_____

_____

_____

_____

_____

GO ON →

4 The following question has two parts. First, answer part A. Then, answer part B.

Part A: Read the stanza from the poem.

They swim as fast as lightning
And protect others in their <u>pod</u>.
Jumping high like shooting stars,
They leave observers awed.

As used in the poem, what is a <u>pod</u>?

(A) a way of moving in the water

(B) a type of jumping

(C) a small group of creatures

(D) a gathering of watchers

Part B: Which phrase from the poem **best** supports your answer in Part A?

(A) They swim

(B) protect others

(C) Jumping high

(D) like shooting stars

GO ON →

5 Read the line from the poem.

A distant sound <u>breaks</u> through the air

What is the **most likely** meaning of the word <u>breaks</u> as used in the poem?

(A) disobeys

(B) fails

(C) splits

(D) stops

6 What are the poet's **most likely** reasons for using first-person point of view? Pick two choices.

(A) to show why the speaker is like a dolphin

(B) to express the speaker's wish to be like a dolphin

(C) to point out why everyone loves to watch dolphins

(D) to show how other animals behave like dolphins

(E) to help readers understand why the speaker likes dolphins

GO ON →

7 The following question has two parts. First, answer part A. Then, answer part B.

Part A: Which sentence provides the **best** summary of the poem?

(A) A young person daydreams about what life would be like as a dolphin.

(B) An observer admires the beauty and graceful movements of dolphins.

(C) A dolphin tries to dance and jump like ballet dancers and acrobats.

(D) A group of people watch the dolphins as the creatures play games with each other.

Part B: Which line from the poem **best** supports your answer in Part A?

(A) Black ocean turns to blue.

(B) As dolphins come into view.

(C) They swim as fast as lightning

(D) These ballet dancers of the sea

GO ON →

Read the passage. Then answer the questions.

A Helping Hand—or Paw?

Most of us realize that animals are fun to watch. Others are fun to have as pets. But did you know animals help humans and the whole planet?

Being of Service

Many animals can be trained as service animals. Dogs are easy to train. They have a very strong sense of smell. They have been used as helpers for people with certain illnesses. The dogs can alert their humans to changes in their bodies that may not be normal. Dogs also are used as guides for people who cannot see or hear well. Dogs sometimes visit places like hospitals. They often help people feel happier.

Monkeys can be service animals also. They help people who have a limited ability to move. One group focuses on training a type of monkey called a capuchin. These monkeys do many tasks that people with various disabilities cannot do. This includes everything from turning off lights and turning on computers to turning the pages of a book.

Keeping Safe

Dogs use their strong sense of smell to sniff out dangerous materials in public places. Other animals use their sense of smell to help too. The African giant pouched rat is trained to sniff out buried explosives. They can find people in buried rubble after a natural disaster. They are even aware of diseases in human spit! Bees can smell land mines and are like helicopters. Because the bees only fly above the mines, they are not in danger of setting them off. Bees also can make specific buzzing sounds when they find dangerous chemicals.

Protecting the Environment

Animals also help protect the earth. One national group puts dogs to work finding where endangered animals and plants are living. The group then tracks and protects these species. Some animals can travel to places that humans cannot. For example, the freezing, deep waters of the Arctic Ocean are dangerous for people. So, scientists have put monitors on the Arctic's

GO ON →

narwhals, elephant seals, and sea lions. The monitors measure the temperature and currents of the ocean. This information helps scientists learn about how the earth's climate is changing.

Animals help keep people safe. They even help protect the environment. Using their unique and special abilities, these incredible animals truly make the world a better place.

GO ON →

8 The following question has two parts. First, answer part A. Then, answer part B.

Part A: According to "A Helping Hand—or Paw," which animal is able to handle extreme temperatures?

Ⓐ the capuchin monkey

Ⓑ the African giant pouched rat

Ⓒ the elephant seal

Ⓓ the honeybee

Part B: Which sentence from the passage **best** supports your answer in Part A?

Ⓐ These monkeys can do many tasks that people with various disabilities cannot do.

Ⓑ They can find people in buried rubble after a natural disaster.

Ⓒ Because the bees only fly above the mines, they are not in danger of setting them off.

Ⓓ So, scientists have put monitors on the Arctic's narwhals, elephant seals, and sea lions.

GO ON →

9 Read the sentence from the passage.

Using their unique and special abilities, these <u>incredible</u> animals truly make the world a better place.

The root word *credible* means "believable." Which is **nearly** the meaning of <u>incredible</u>?

(A) very unusual and fascinating

(B) completely true and based on facts

(C) often imagined but accepted as real

(D) totally understood by almost everyone

10 Draw a line to match **each** detail from the passage to the main idea that it supports.

Animals help protect the planet.

Animals help people.

Sea animals wear devices to monitor the ocean's currents.

Monkeys can turn off lights and turn pages in a book.

Dogs go where endangered animals are living.

Dogs can sniff out dangerous things in public places.

Bees buzz when they smell dangerous chemicals.

GO ON →

11 According to the passage, how do animals use their sense of smell to help people? Pick **three** choices.

(A) They notice changes in people's bodies that people may not be aware of.

(B) They switch lights and computers on and off whenever needed.

(C) They find dangerous materials and explosives in a variety of places.

(D) They explore locations known for extreme temperatures.

(E) They wear monitors that measure ocean temperatures and currents.

(F) They visit hospitals to cheer up patients and make them happier.

(G) They find people who have been buried under rubble after natural disasters.

12 Read the sentence from the passage.

Bees can smell land mines and are like helicopters.

Explain what **two** things are being compared in the sentence and how the comparison helps the reader understand how a bee flies over land mines.

_____

_____

_____

_____

_____

GO ON →

13 The following question has two parts. First, answer part A. Then, answer part B.

Part A: Which structure does the author **mostly** use in the passage?

(A) a description of problems and how animals provide the solutions

(B) a comparison of how different types of animals help people in trouble

(C) a timeline of how animals and insects have helped people over the years

(D) an explanation of how disasters are caused and the effects animals have on them

Part B: Which sentence from the passage **best** supports your answer in Part A?

(A) Most of us realize that animals are fun to watch.

(B) The dogs can alert their humans to changes in their bodies that may not be normal.

(C) Monkeys can be service animals also.

(D) Other animals use their sense of smell to help too.

GO ON →

Name: _____ Date: _____

14 The following question has two parts. First, answer part A. Then, answer part B.

Part A: Read the sentence from the passage.

These monkeys do many tasks that people with various <u>disabilities</u> cannot do.

Which word has **most nearly** the opposite meaning from <u>disabilities</u>?

(A) need

(B) power

(C) support

(D) teaching

Part B: Which statement from the passage **best** supports your answer in Part A?

(A) Monkeys can be service animals also.

(B) They help people who have a limited ability to move.

(C) One group focuses on training a type of monkey called a capuchin.

(D) This includes everything from turning off lights and turning on computers to turning the pages of a book.

GO ON →

Read the passages. Then answer the questions.

How Animals Use Tools

Tools are usually thought of as human inventions. But did you know that animals use tools to solve problems, too?

The chimpanzee, for example, uses grass stems to catch termites. This animal knows where these insects live. It pokes a stem into the termites' nest. Then it waits. Inside the nest, the termites crawl over the stem. The chimpanzee pulls out the termite-covered stem and licks it clean. This is a good meal for a chimpanzee.

Sometimes the chimpanzee has trouble locating water. When this happens, it often uses leaves as a tool. The chimpanzee pushes leaves into places that it cannot reach. The leaves soak up the water from these places. Then the chimpanzee chews on the leaves. Chimps have also been known to use sticks as digging tools.

The woodpecker finch is another animal that uses tools. It uses small sticks to pick insects out of tree bark. Another animal that uses tools is the sea otter. It uses rocks to crack open shellfish. Here is how. The otter places the rock on its chest. Then it holds the shellfish in its paws and bangs it against the rock. This cracks the shell open and allows the otter to eat the creature inside.

The green heron uses bait to catch fish, just as humans use bait on the end of a fishing pole. The heron does this by picking up a small object with its beak. It flies over the water and drops the object onto the surface. Beneath the water, fish see the object and swim toward it. The

This chimpanzee uses a stick as a tool to dig for termites.

GO ON →

heron waits for fish to swim close to the surface. Then it swoops down and snaps up the fish.

Some animals have uses for tools other than gathering food and water. Some use leaves to dab at wounds or to clean. Some even use twigs as toothpicks. A scientist named Benjamin Beck discovered that crows are very good at solving problems. One unusual crow that lived in Beck's lab ate dry food moistened with a little water. When people forgot to add water to the food, the bird used a cup and added its own water.

The elephant is one of the most intelligent animals. Using its trunk as an arm, the elephant puts grass and branches together. It then uses this tool to swat flies. When needed, this tool can also be used as a back scratcher.

Let's not forget the amazing bottle-nosed dolphins. These remarkable animals twist sea sponges around their snouts. Why? Dolphins hunt the ocean's bottom-dwellers. They use their snouts to turn up sediment and find food. Sometimes they scrape their snouts on sand, rocks, shells, and other objects. Covering their snouts with sponges helps them avoid scrapes, or worse still, stings from poisonous animals.

These are just a few examples of how animals use tools. Scientists are discovering more and more every day. Every time scientists see animals using tools, it makes them rethink their ideas about animal behavior.

GO ON →

Meeting Cody

It was a cool fall day, and the air was as crisp as apple cider. Andy was doing exactly what he liked best—racing his bicycle as fast as it would go.

As he sped along the sidewalk, the wind brushed against his face like a cool, refreshing spray. It had been a good day. At school, he had given his science report on pandas, and everyone seemed to like it. Then, at recess, he had scored two goals in the soccer game. Yes, today life was very good.

As he rounded the corner he saw the bright yellow caution tape and the orange cones in front of Mrs. Alemu's house. His mom had already warned him to stay away from the big hole in the sidewalk. "If you fell in that hole, you could be seriously injured, so it is best to just steer clear of it altogether," she had suggested.

The hole did not seem that deep, thought Andy, peering over the edge. If he went fast enough, surely he would be able to jump it without any problem. He made up his mind to give it a try and moved the cones over to Mrs. Alemu's yard. Getting back on his bicycle, Andy pedaled as fast as he could, feeling like a train thundering down the sidewalk.

As he neared the hole, his mom's warning echoed louder in his head. Maybe she was right; he might get hurt. "Mom will be really disappointed in me if I do this," Andy thought. At the last minute, he changed his mind and turned his bike's front wheel onto the grass to avoid hitting the hole. Instead, he crashed into the orange cones and fell to the sidewalk.

* * *

It had been a week since Andy had broken his leg, and he had spent all of it lying on the couch or in his room.

"Hey, Andy," his dad said walking into the room. "Your buddies are here to see you!" When Andy sighed, his father added, "Give them a chance—they just want to check on you."

As his friends piled through the doorway, they could tell Andy was upset but hoped that playing a card game would cheer him up. It did not take long to realize that even cards were not helping, and finally, Andy pretended to be tired so the boys would leave.

GO ON →

For the next week, Andy continued to feel sorry for himself. Then one day he woke to wet sandpaper dragging across his face. He opened his eyes to see a dog staring him in the face, with its tongue hanging out. "Surprise!" his parents yelled.

"Great, now the dog can feel sorry for me too," Andy said, wiping his cheek with his sleeve.

"Dogs don't feel sorry for people—only people do that," his father said. "We thought adopting this guy would help get you out of this fog you have been in."

"Whatever," Andy said without much interest. When the dog just sat there staring at him, Andy quietly asked, "What's his name?"

"We named him Cody," his mom replied. "Now Dad and I will let you two get to know each other," she said as they left the room.

After a few minutes Cody nudged Andy's hand with his nose, and Andy had to smile. Maybe having a dog would be better than he had thought. "You want to go outside, Cody?" Andy asked. Cody jumped up excitedly, and carefully, Andy stood up too. He hobbled to the back door on his crutches and, as he and Cody passed through the kitchen, Andy's mom whispered, "Well, will you look at that?"

As Andy sat on the porch steps, he said, "You know, boy, Dad said only people feel sorry for themselves." He paused and leaned down to pick up a stick. "I've spent a lot of time feeling sorry for myself, but that's going to change now," he said, throwing the stick across the yard. Cody dashed after it but turned to bark at his new friend. Andy was almost sure he was saying, "Welcome back!"

GO ON →

Answer these questions about "How Animals Use Tools."

15 The following question has two parts. First, answer part A. Then, answer part B.

Part A: Which animal uses a tool in almost the same way as the chimpanzee?

(A) the woodpecker finch

(B) the sea otter

(C) the green heron

(D) the bottle-nosed dolphin

Part B: Which sentence from the passage supports your answer in Part A?

(A) First, the otter places the rock on its chest.

(B) It uses small sticks to pick insects out of tree bark.

(C) The green heron uses bait to catch fish just as humans use bait on the end of a fishing pole to attract fish.

(D) By covering their snouts in sponges, they can avoid getting hurt, or getting stung by the ocean's poisonous animals.

GO ON →

16 Read the sentence from the passage.

> **One <u>unusual</u> crow that lived in Beck's lab ate dry food moistened with a little water.**

The prefix un- means "not" or "the opposite of." Which is **nearly** the meaning of <u>unusual</u>?

(A) popular

(B) pretty

(C) rare

(D) strong

17 Explain how the image and caption help the reader better understand the ideas in the passage. Use **two** details from the passage to support your answer.

_____

_____

_____

_____

_____

GO ON →

Answer these questions about "Meeting Cody."

18 Which sentence **best** states the main theme of the passage "Meeting Cody"?

(A) Life is nearly impossible to predict.

(B) Follow safety rules when riding a bicycle.

(C) Surprises can often be more fun than you would think.

(D) Feeling sorry for yourself does not improve a situation.

19 Read the sentence from the passage.

Then one day, he woke to wet sandpaper dragging across his face.

Describe what two things are being compared. Then explain how the comparison helps the reader understand the author's idea.

_____

_____

_____

_____

_____

_____

GO ON →

20 The following question has two parts. First, answer part A. Then, answer part B.

Part A: Which sentence provides the **best** summary of the passage?

(A) A boy gets hurt when he makes a mistake, and then almost makes a bigger one with self-pity.

(B) A dog finds the perfect home to live in because a boy is feeling very lonely and missing his friends.

(C) A city street is full of danger, and when a boy does not pay attention to the warnings, he is seriously hurt.

(D) A family finds a way to show their son that following the rules is the most important lesson to learn.

Part B: Which sentence from the passage **best** supports your answer in Part A?

(A) "We thought adopting this guy would help get you out of this fog you have been in."

(B) It had been a week since Andy had broken his leg, and he had spent all of it lying on the couch or in his room.

(C) Maybe having a dog would be better than he had thought.

(D) "I've spent a lot of time feeling sorry for myself, but that's going to change now," he said, throwing the stick across the yard.

GO ON →

Now answer this question about "How Animals Use Tools" and "Meeting Cody."

21 "How Animals Use Tools" showed how animals use items like sticks, leaves, rocks, and sponges for a number of purposes. In "Meeting Cody," Andy used a variety of tools, such as his bicycle and his crutches. Contrast the purposes of both sets of tools. Support your answer with clear evidence from both passages.

_____

_____

_____

_____

_____

_____

_____

_____

_____

_____

_____

_____

_____

_____

GO ON →

The passage below needs revision. Read the passage. Then answer the questions.

I've always loved animals, but we can't have a dog or cat because my brother is allergic to animal fur. My mother loves animals too. She works as a volunteer at a local ___(1)___ . My ___(2)___ job sounds really fun.

Mom has told me many ___(3)___ about the animals at the shelter. I'm still too young to volunteer, but last week I asked my mom if I could go with her to help. She told me I could but warned me to be ready to work. ___(4)___ jobs can change every day. Most of the time, Mom helps socialize the cats. This means that she helps cats get used to people so they can be adopted and have better ___(5)___ . We spent all afternoon "socializing" the cats.

GO ON →

22 Which answer should go in blank (1)?

(A) Animal Shelter

(B) Animal shelter

(C) animal shelter

23 Which answer should go in blank (2)?

(A) mothers'

(B) mother's

(C) mothers

24 Which answer should go in blank (3)?

(A) stories

(B) storyes

(C) storys

25 Which answer should go in blank (4)?

(A) Volunteer's

(B) Volunteers'

(C) Volunteers

26 Which answer should go in blank (5)?

(A) lifes

(B) life

(C) lives

GO ON →

The passage below needs revision. Read the passage. Then answer the questions.

Big Cats

(1) Big cats are large. (2) They are also powerful. (3) They are much bigger and stronger than household cats. (4) Lions cheetahs and leopards are big cats.

(5) Many big cats live in the grasslands of africa. (6) The cheetah, the world's fastest land mammal, is one. (7) It can run 70 miles per hour. (8) It has excellent eyesight. (9) The cheetah's spotted coat helps it blend into the high grass. (10) It also has long, sharp tooths. (11) Most of the time, the cheetah's prey does not see the cheetah until it is far too late.

GO ON →

27 What is the **best** way to combine sentences 1 and 2 without changing the meaning?

Ⓐ Big cats are large and big cats are powerful.

Ⓑ Cats are big and powerful and large.

Ⓒ Powerful and large are the cats.

Ⓓ Big cats are large and powerful.

28 What is the correct way to write sentence 4?

Ⓐ Lions, cheetahs, and leopards are big cats.

Ⓑ Lions cheetahs, and leopards are big cats.

Ⓒ Lions, cheetahs, and, leopards are big cats.

Ⓓ Lions, cheetahs, and leopards, are big cats.

29 What is the correct way to write sentence 5?

Ⓐ Many big cats live in the grasslands of Africa.

Ⓑ Many big cats live in the Grasslands of africa.

Ⓒ Many big cats live in the Grasslands of Africa.

Ⓓ Many big Cats live in the Grasslands of Africa.

GO ON →

30 What is the **best** way to combine sentences 7 and 8 without changing the meaning?

Ⓐ It can run 70 miles per hour although it has excellent eyesight.

Ⓑ It can run 70 miles per hour since it has excellent eyesight.

Ⓒ It can run 70 miles per hour and has excellent eyesight.

Ⓓ It can run 70 mile per hour, but it has excellent eyesight.

31 What is the correct way to write sentence 10?

Ⓐ It also has long, sharp tooth.

Ⓑ It also has long, sharp toothes.

Ⓒ It also has long, sharp teeth.

Ⓓ It also has long, sharp teeths.

Informational Performance Task

Task:

Your class has been learning about animals and how amazing they are. Now your class is going to create a website to share what they have learned. Each student will write something for the website.

Before you decide what you will write about animals, you do some research and find two articles that provide information about how animals communicate, or "talk" to each other. After you have looked at these sources, you will answer some questions about them. Briefly scan the sources and the three questions that follow. Then, go back and read the sources carefully to gain the information you will need to answer the questions and write an informational article for the class website.

In Part 2, you will write your article using information from the two sources.

Directions for Part 1

You will now look at two sources. You can look at either of the sources as often as you like.

Research Questions:

After looking at the sources, use the rest of the time in Part 1 to answer three questions about them. Your answers to these questions will be scored. Also, your answers will help you think about the information you have read, which should help you write your informational article. You may refer to the sources when you think it would be helpful. You may also look at your notes.

GO ON →

Source 1: Can Animals Talk?

People share thoughts and feelings using words. How about animals? Many people think that animals cannot communicate with each other. After all, only humans use words. However, we can also tell each other things without words. We wave our hands to 'say' hello and goodbye. We smile, frown and raise our eyebrows to share how we feel and what we think. Believe it or not, some animals can also tell each other many things without using words. Here are a few examples.

Animal Sounds

Animals do not use words or language, but they do make many kinds of sounds. These sounds tell other animals things they need to know. Robins find each other using chirps and songs. Cobras hiss warnings. Blue whales sing low, loud notes to call out to other whales. Scientists now understand that animal songs can vary depending on where each animal lives. So animals can have different accents!

Vervet monkeys warn other monkeys using special sounds. A "cough call" means danger overhead. When the monkeys hear the cough call, they take cover under bushes and look to the skies and hide from flying predators like eagles. But Vervet monkeys give a completely different warning sound if danger comes on land, such as an oncoming leopard.

Peacocks use their tail feathers to make special sounds, which are so low that human ears cannot hear them! But peahens (female peacocks) can hear them. When they hear tail feathers rustle, they come to see what all the noise is about.

Animal Gestures

Many animals communicate using body language. In Rwanda's Volcanoes National Park, gorillas beat their chests. Are they angry? No, they are happy and letting the other gorillas know how they feel. Dogs let people and other animals know they are happy by wagging their tails. Animals can also send warnings with body language. When cats arch their backs, they are saying, "Stay away!"

GO ON →

Many animals also reach out to express themselves. Chimpanzees help groom their friends. Using their hands, they pat their friends on the back and help keep their fur clean. Grooming leads to cooperation and sharing in the group. This sends the message that they are friends.

Even animals in the seas use touch to tell how they are feeling. Sea otters rub noses with each other. They may even touch noses with other animals like seals and sea lions! This "nosing around" signals play and trust.

So, can animals actually talk? The short answer is 'no.' Only humans can use words as language. However, animals communicate in many ways. The more we study animals, the more we learn about other methods of communication.

Source 2: Sneaky Animal Signals

Many animals communicate with sights and sounds. Dogs wag their tails. Chickens strut. Pigs grunt. Cats meow. But did you know that some animals can give and receive messages in ways we cannot? Some animals use their powers of touch, taste, and smell to send and receive signals that we can't even sense. How sneaky!

Charged with Feeling

Did you know that some types of fish use electricity to communicate? Some fish send electrical pulses that bounce back to them and tell them where good food is. Other fish, like sharks, for example, can feel the electrical signals of their prey. This way, they can "feel" where their food is. The electrical pulses are not dangerous. They are weak electrical signals that cannot hurt other animals or people. We can't even feel them. Electrical signaling is an ideal type of communication for animals that live in dark, unclear waters.

Chemical Tastes and Smells

Some animals can detect chemical cues that we can't sense at all. Snakes can use their special forked tongues to "taste" the scent of animals in the air. Snakes can tell which chemical cues belong to dangerous animals and which come from animals that would make a good dinner. Snakes have receptors in the roofs of their mouths that help them sense the chemical cues of animals nearby.

GO ON →

Have you ever smelled skunk spray? Skunks spray a stinky odor to protect themselves from predators like bears that otherwise would try to eat them! Some animals have scents they use to communicate that we can't detect at all. Have you ever seen a cat rub its head against something? It is marking its territory. Cats have scent glands near their mouths, on their foreheads, and at the base of their tails. They use these organs to mark territory and tell other cats to stay away. Insects communicate with scents, too. Some moths make special chemicals that other moths can sense to find them.

Many animals say things through songs, growls, and whistles. But it is amazing to know that some animals send signals that no one can hear. They can send these signals in daylight or the dark of night. They learn things this way. Animals have a lot to say. We just don't always understand how they say it. Scientists are working to learn more about animals and the incredible signals they use.

GO ON →

Name: _____ Date: _____

1 Match each detail to the source or sources in which the detail is given. Draw a line from **each** detail to its source.

Source 1: Can Animals Talk?   Pulses of electricity can help in finding food.

Source 2: Sneaky Animal Signals   Senses help animals communicate.

Both Source 1 and Source 2   Sounds can warn of danger.

2 Read the sentence from "Sneaky Animal Signals."

But it is amazing to know that some animals send signals that no one can hear.

What details from each source support this sentence? Use **one** detail from **each** source to support your explanation. Be sure to give the source number or title for each detail.

_____

_____

_____

_____

_____

GO ON →

Name: _____ Date: _____

3 Both "Can Animals Talk?" and "Sneaky Animal Signals" give information about how animals send messages.

Explain what you have learned about how animals send messages. Use **one** detail from **each** source to support your explanation. Be sure to give the source number or title for each detail.

_____

_____

_____

_____

_____

GO ON →

Directions for Part 2

You will now look at your sources, take notes, and plan, draft, revise, and edit your article for the website. First read your assignment and the information about how your informational article will be scored. Then begin your work.

Your Assignment:

Your class is creating a website about amazing things animals can do. For your part of the website, you will write an informational article about how animals "talk" to other animals. Your article will be read by other students, teachers, parents, and other people who visit the website.

Using information from the two sources, "Can Animals Talk?" and "Sneaky Animal Signals," develop a main idea about how animals communicate. Choose the most important information from more than one source to support your main idea. Then, write an informational article several paragraphs long. Clearly organize your article and support your main idea with details from the sources.

Use your own words except when quoting directly from the sources. Be sure to give the source title when using details from the sources.

REMEMBER: A well-written informational article

- has a clear main idea
- is well-organized and stays on the topic
- has an introduction and conclusion
- uses transitions
- uses details from the sources to support the main idea
- develops ideas fully
- uses clear language
- follows rules of writing (spelling, punctuation, and grammar)

Now begin work on your informational article. Manage your time carefully so that you can plan, write, revise, and edit the final draft of your article. Write your response on a separate sheet of paper.

Question	Correct Answer	Content Focus	CCSS	Complexity
1	see below	Context Clues: Antonyms	L.4.5c	DOK 2
2A	D	Theme	RL.4.2	DOK 3
2B	C	Theme/Text Evidence	RL.4.2/ RL.4.1	DOK 3
3	see below	Point of View	RL.4.6	DOK 3
4A	C	Context Clues: Sentence Clues	L.4.4a	DOK 2
4B	B	Context Clues: Sentence Clues/Text Evidence	L.4.4a/ RL.4.1	DOK 2
5	C	Context Clues: Multiple-Meaning Words	L.4.4a	DOK 2
6	B, E	Point of View	RL.4.6	DOK 3
7A	B	Theme	RL.4.2	DOK 3
7B	D	Theme/Text Evidence	RL.4.2/ RL.4.1	DOK 3
8A	C	Main Idea and Key Details	RI.4.2	DOK 2
8B	D	Main Idea and Key Details/Text Evidence	RI.4.1/ RI.4.2	DOK 2
9	A	Prefixes	L.4.4b	DOK 2
10	see below	Main Idea and Key Details	RI.4.2	DOK 2
11	A, C, G	Main Idea and Key Details	RI.4.2	DOK 2
12	see below	Figurative Language: Similes and Metaphors	L.4.5a	DOK 3
13A	A	Text Structure: Problem and Solution	RI.4.5	DOK 3
13B	B	Text Structure: Problem and Solution/Text Evidence	RI.4.5/ RI.4.1	DOK 3
14A	B	Context Clues: Antonyms	L.4.4a	DOK 2
14B	B	Context Clues: Antonyms/Text Evidence	L.4.4a/ RL.4.1	DOK 2
15A	A	Main Idea and Key Details	RI.4.2	DOK 3
15B	B	Main Idea and Key Details/Text Evidence	RI.4.1/ RI.4.2	DOK 3
16	C	Prefixes	L.4.4b	DOK 2
17	see below	Text Features: Images with Captions	RI.4.7	DOK 3
18	D	Theme	RL.4.2	DOK 3
19	see below	Figurative Language: Similes and Metaphors	RL.4.5	DOK 3

Name: _____

Question	Correct Answer	Content Focus	CCSS	Complexity
20A	A	Theme	RL.4.2	DOK 3
20B	D	Theme/Text Evidence	RL.4.2/ RL.4.1	DOK 3
21	see below	Compare Across Texts	W.4.9	DOK 4
22	C	Common and Proper Nouns	L.4.2a	DOK 1
23	B	Possessive Nouns	L.3.2d	DOK 1
24	A	Singular and Plural Nouns	L.3.1b	DOK 1
25	B	Possessive Nouns	L.3.2d	DOK 1
26	C	Irregular Plural Nouns	L.3.1b	DOK 1
27	D	Combining Sentences	L.3.1.h/ L.3.1.i	DOK 1
28	A	Punctuation, Comma Use	L.4.2(a-d)	DOK 1
29	A	Common and Proper Nouns: Capitalization	L.4.2a	DOK 1
30	C	Combining Sentences	L.3.1h/ L.3.1i	DOK 2
31	C	Irregular Plural Nouns	L.3.1b	DOK 1

Comprehension: Selected Response 2A, 2B, 6A, 6B, 7A, 7B, 8A, 8B, 11, 13A, 13B, 15A, 15B, 18, 20A, 20B	/18	%
Comprehension: Constructed Response 3, 10, 17, 21	/10	%
Vocabulary 1, 4A, 4B, 5, 9, 12, 14A, 14B, 16, 19	/16	%
English Language Conventions 22–31	/10	%
Total Unit Assessment Score	/54	%

1 Students should draw lines to match the following:
  • recedes: advances
  • recedes: approaches

3 **2-point response:** The speaker compares dolphins to birds, to lightning, to shooting stars, and to ballet dancers. These comparisons suggest that dolphins are graceful in their leaping and "dancing," fast-moving, and wonderful to watch.

10 Students should draw lines to match the following:
- Animals help protect the planet: Sea animals wear devices to monitor the ocean's currents.
- Animals help protect the planet: Dogs go where endangered animals are living.
- Animals help people: Monkeys can turn off lights and turn pages in a book.
- Animals help people: Dogs can sniff out dangerous things in public places.

12 **2-point response:** Bees and helicopters are being compared. The comparison suggests the bee hovers over the area where landmines are located, like a helicopter would hover.

17 **2-point response:** This image shows a chimpanzee using a stick as a tool. It is an example of what the passage describes in words, and it helps readers visualize the action.

20 **2-point response:** A dog's tongue is being compared to wet sandpaper. The comparison helps the reader understand how the dog's tongue felt when the puppy licked him.

21 **4-point response:** People and animals use and need tools to do things they cannot do without help. In "Meeting Cody," tools are used to help people move, to warn of dangers, and as toys. The animals in "How Animals Use Tools" include a chimpanzee that uses a stick to gather termites and leaves to get water, a woodpecker finch that uses a stick to reach bugs, a green heron that uses bait to catch fish, an elephant that uses grass to swat flies, and a bottle-nosed dolphin that uses a sponge to protect its snout. "How Animals Use Tools" explains how the animals use tools for survival, specifically to get food and water.

Answer Key   Name: _____

Informational Performance Task				
Question	**Answer**	**CCSS**	**Complexity**	**Score**
1	see below		DOK 3	/1
2	see below	RI.4.1, RI.4.2, RI.4.9 W.4.2a-e, W.4.4, W.4.7 L.4.1, L.4.2	DOK 3	/2
3	see below		DOK 3	/2
Informational Article	see below		DOK 4	/4 [P/O] /4 [E/E] /2 [C]
Total Score				/15

1 Students should draw lines to match the following statements:
• Source 1: Can Animals Talk?: Sounds can warn of danger.
• Source 2: Sneaky Animal Signals: Pulses of electricity can help in finding food.
• Both Source 1 and Source 2: Senses help animals communicate.

2 **2-point response:** Some animals send signals that no one can hear. In Source #2 we learned that sharks detect their prey by feeling the electrical signals. They can "feel" where their food is. In Source #1, we learned that male peacocks communicate by rustling their feathers to attract a mate. The sound they make is so low a human is unable to hear it.

3 **2-point response:** Both sources discuss how animals can communicate by sending special messages. In Source #2, we learned that cats have special glands on their foreheads near their mouths and at the base of their tail to mark their territory with a special scent. In Source #1, we learned that Vervet monkeys use special sounds, including one that sounds like a cough, to warn other monkeys that dangerous predators are near.

10-point anchor paper: Have you ever wondered how animals "talk" to each other? Do they communicate like we do? Many scientists have spent time studying animals and have discovered that animals do not communicate using language like humans do. Humans communicate using speech, or writing. If they have a need, or want to tell a friend something, they use language to communicate. However, animals can "talk" to each other in other ways. They use communicate using methods such as sight, smell, touch, and even body language.

One way is sound. According to Source #1, animals use sounds to tell other animals things they need to know. One animal, the Vervet monkey, uses a special sound like a cough to warn other monkeys in their group of danger from above. The "cough call" tells the other monkeys to hide under a bush because a predator, like an Eagle, is in the sky. The monkeys make a different noise when others are in danger from a predator on the ground.

Taste is another sense that animals use to communicate with each other. According to Source #2, a snake has an unusual way of detecting animals nearby. They have a special tongue to "taste" the air. By detecting the scent of other animals, they can tell if they are good to eat or dangerous and they need to stay away from them.

Animals also can communicate through the use of body language. According to source #1, some animals use body language to express their feelings to other animals. A gorilla will beat its chest and a dog will wag its tail when they are happy. A cat will tell you it is not happy by arching its back and hissing.

Some animals have a unique way to communicate using the sense of touch. According to Source #2, some animals use electricity to sense where they can find food. They send electric pulses that will bounce back to them informing them where to look for food. They can "feel" exactly where to look. This is helpful, especially if animals hunt in areas with little light.

The skunk and cat even have a unique way of communicating with other animals—through scent. According to Source #2, skunks will spray a stinky smell to let other animals know to stay away! Cats have a scent that humans cannot detect, but other animals can. They have special glands in their heads, and tails that they will rub on objects to mark their territory. Other animals can detect this scent, and know that they need to stay away from that area.

In conclusion, animals do not communicate with each other like humans do, but they have a lot to say! According to Source #1 and Source #2, researchers continue to study animals and the way they communicate. They hope to further understand the great things animals have to say.

Read the passage. Then answer the questions.

Critter Crossing

Our teacher, Mr. Singh, has a class project that requires us to become involved in something to help our community, so he assigned us to small groups to talk about our ideas. Mr. Singh told us that each group would need to come up with an idea for a project to present to the class. After all of the ideas are presented, then the whole class will vote to choose one project we want to complete together.

I took one look at my group and felt a black cloud of doom start to gather. First in the group was Max. Actually, Max is my friend, but he is completely obsessed with science, which is not really my thing. One of his birthday presents was a microscope, and he thinks it is the most fascinating object in the universe. He can sit at the microscope for hours watching tiny creatures squirm around in a drop of water.

The next member of the group was Iman. All she ever thinks about is animals. She even has a lot of pets at home, which would not be a good thing for me. I usually avoid animals because it seems as though I am allergic to every imaginable kind of animal.

Finally, there was Cally. She is constantly drawing and sketching, and she doesn't talk much. She can usually be found sitting somewhere drawing and doodling, which can become annoying if you are hoping to find someone to talk with or do something with after school.

As for me, just get me outdoors! That's all I ask. Whether I am simply bicycling with my friends, walking around town, or playing ball in the park, I am just happy to be outside.

When we sat down to talk about project ideas, Iman started the discussion about what we could do.

"I think our project should be to volunteer at the animal shelter," she said. "It's a great way to contribute to the community, and it will be fun. Of course, that's just one suggestion. I'm going to write down everybody's ideas. But, Theo," she added, staring straight at me, "I really don't think the town needs a new baseball diamond."

GO ON →

Amazing! How did she know what I was going to suggest?

Then Max spoke up. "What about helping wild animals?" he said. Cally started sketching a tiger on her notepad. "I just learned that there is a zoologist at the nature center who we could help. She has been working to save animals on the road by Warner's Woods, because the traffic on that road is causing big problems for the wildlife." He glanced at Cally's notepad. "Sorry, Cally," he said. "I'm talking about helping amphibians and reptiles. Not that I wouldn't help tigers if I could!"

"So, what is your suggestion? What are you proposing?" asked Iman.

"Cars and trucks are killing a lot of animals. Spotted salamanders and Blanding's turtles are especially vulnerable because they need to cross the road to get to their nesting grounds. Maybe we could help protect these critters from harm," Max finished.

"We could start a campaign to inform more people about the problem. We could also put signs along the road that would tell people to watch out for turtles and salamanders," suggested Cally.

"Sure," Max agreed. "The zoologist said the spotted salamanders cross the road in huge numbers on the first rainy night in early March. Every year, people from the nature center go out with flashlights and buckets to help them cross safely."

"Maybe some of us could help with that, too," I suggested.

This idea was beginning to sound interesting. We did some research and found pictures of spotted salamanders and Blanding's turtles. Iman immediately fell in love with them, and Cally started designing a "Critter Crossing" sign.

"What would really help the animals is to have a tunnel under the road just for them," said Max excitedly. "Maybe we could get the town to build one. That would be the best way for the turtles and salamanders to cross safely."

Our group of four agreed that Max's "Critter Crossing" project was a great idea that could be a big help for our community. Now we would just have to convince the rest of our class that our project was the best!

GO ON →

1 The following question has two parts. First, answer part A. Then, answer part B.

Part A: Which of these statements **best** shows the meaning of <u>microscope</u> as it is used in the passage?

Ⓐ a tool to measure time

Ⓑ a way to cause motion

Ⓒ a tool to view small objects

Ⓓ a way to draw large objects

Part B: Which statement from the passage **best** supports your answer in part A?

Ⓐ "... thinks it is the most fascinating object in the universe."

Ⓑ "... watching tiny creatures squirm around in a drop of water."

Ⓒ "... playing ball in the park..."

Ⓓ "... started sketching a tiger..."

GO ON →

2 The following question has two parts. First, answer part A. Then, answer part B.

Part A: Read the paragraph from the passage and answer the question.

"So, what is your suggestion? What are you proposing?" asked Iman.

Which word is a synonym of proposing?

(A) asking

(B) demanding

(C) guessing

(D) offering

Part B: Which sentence from the passage **best** supports your answer in part A?

(A) "Not that I wouldn't help tigers if I could!"

(B) "Cars and trucks are killing a lot of animals."

(C) "Spotted salamanders and Blanding's turtles are especially vulnerable because they need to cross the road to get to their nesting grounds."

(D) "'Maybe we could help protect these critters from harm,' Max finished."

GO ON →

3 The following question has two parts. First, answer part A. Then, answer part B.

Part A: Which statement **best** explains how the narrator shows that Iman knows him well?

(A) Iman is the note taker for the group.

(B) Iman is friends with the group members.

(C) Iman is aware of the interests of each group member.

(D) Iman is certain he will suggest something to do with sports.

Part B: Which sentence from the passage **best** supports your answer in part A?

(A) "All she ever thinks about is animals."

(B) "I'm going to write down everybody's ideas."

(C) "How did she know what I was going to suggest?"

(D) "'What about helping wild animals?' he said."

GO ON →

4 The following question has two parts. First, answer part A. Then, answer part B.

Part A: What does Cally **most likely** believe?

(A) Every family should have at least one pet.

(B) Art is often better than words for expressing ideas.

(C) Studying the world around you is often worthwhile.

(D) The school schedule should allow plenty of time for sports.

Part B: Which detail from the passage **best** supports your answer in Part A?

(A) "he is completely obsessed with science."

(B) "has a lot of pets at home"

(C) "constantly drawing and sketching"

(D) "the town needs a new baseball diamond."

GO ON →

5 Which part of the project should Cally be in charge of, and which part of the project should Max be in charge of?

Draw a line to match **one** phrase for Cally and **one** phrase for Max from the list.

Cally   choosing helpers

Max   making signs

                         naming the animals

                         finding animal foster care

                         researching the topic

                         developing rules

6 Read the sentences from the passage.

"I just learned there's a zoologist at the nature center who we could help. She has been working to save animals on the road by Warner's Woods, because the traffic on that road is causing big problems for the wildlife."

Which word from the passage **best** shows what a zoologist studies?

(A) center

(B) animals

(C) road

(D) problems

GO ON →

7 Why would Iman **most likely** think that the Critter Crossing project is a good idea? Use details from the passage to support your answer.

_____

_____

_____

_____

_____

_____

Read the passage. Then answer the questions.

A Random Act of Sewing

Every day, she gathers her scissors and pins and picks out a colorful piece of fabric. By now, she certainly knows the patterns by heart. Next, she measures and cuts carefully. Then she sits down in front of her sewing machine. Soon, the thread begins to fly.

Lillian Weber is a wonderful seamstress. She has spent her life with a needle and thread in her hand. She began stitching when she was only eight years old and has never stopped. Her years of practice have made her talented—and fast. In just four hours, she can turn a piece of material into a lovely dress. She starts in the morning and works until lunch. After a break, she returns to the project, and by dinner, she is done. Weber makes a dress every single day and has done so for the past three years. In that time, she has made almost 900 dresses. Her goal is to make 1,000 dresses by her birthday in May 2015. This is a great goal, especially considering that on that day, Weber will also turn 100 years old.

Each morning, the sound of a sewing machine fills Weber's farmhouse in the town of Bettendorf, Iowa. When Weber is done at the sewing machine, she moves over to a comfortable chair. She picks up the needle again to finish the dress she started that morning. When she puts the finishing touches on a dress, she takes extra time to make each one special. One dress gets a unique pattern of stitching. Another dress gets a colorful patch. Bright pockets are added on the front of another dress. She wants each dress to look pretty. She wants each girl who wears one of her dresses to wear it proudly. She knows how important it is to have a piece of clothing that is not like everyone else's.

GO ON →

Weber's dresses are part of "Little Dresses for Africa," an organization that sends clothing to girls in need all over the world. Since the group started, it has sent more than 2.5 million dresses to children in 81 different countries, including the United States. The dresses are handed out in schools and orphanages. Now and then, Weber is able to see photographs of the young girls who have received her dresses. Seeing the happiness in the girls' smiles as they show off their new dresses is more than enough reward for this kind seamstress.

Weber learned about the group from her friend, Judy. In turn, Judy had heard about it on a television show. Judy gathered her friends together and told them about it. The women all decided to start making dresses. Almost every seamstress in the group is over the age of 80.

The story of Lillian Weber's dedication has spread across the world as quickly as her dresses have. Weber is sometimes referred to as the "Sewing Celebrity." She won a local award as part of a TV series in Moline, Iowa, called "Pay It Forward." The TV series focuses on honoring those people who are providing assistance to others and making a positive difference in the world—like Weber. Since then, news reporters in France, Germany, and Japan, and other countries, have been talking about this hard-working woman. It is a story that brings a smile to most people's faces.

What does the 99-year-old woman plan to do when she hits her 100th birthday and makes her 1000th dress? According to Weber, nothing will change. She plans to keep making dresses as long as she can. She has the fabric and the time. Most of all, sewing for others is what she does, and it is certainly what she loves.

GO ON →

8 The following question has two parts. First, answer part A. Then, answer part B.

Part A: Read the sentence from the passage.

Lillian Weber is a wonderful <u>seamstress</u>.

What does a <u>seamstress</u> do?

(A) cares about other people

(B) lives to be almost 100 years old

(C) makes items by sewing

(D) comes from the state of Iowa

Part B: Which words from the passage provide the **best** clue to the meaning of <u>seamstress</u>?

(A) "... needle and thread ..."

(B) "... years of practice ..."

(C) "... farmhouse in the town ..."

(D) "... seeing the happiness ..."

GO ON →

9 Draw lines to match **three** reasons why the author **most likely** includes the information about Lillian Weber's age.

reason to include
Weber's age

to suggest that she has done many other things besides sewing

reason to include
Weber's age

to emphasize how unusual it is for a person her age to be this active

reason to include
Weber's age

to reveal why she likes receiving photographs of girls wearing her dresses

to point out that many people her age enjoy hobbies

to show how she is different from the typical seamstress

to explain why she is so good at sewing

to highlight her energy and dedication to helping others

GO ON →

10 The following question has two parts. First, answer part A. Then, answer part B.

Part A: How does the author show that Weber pays great attention to detail?

(A) by showing how Weber works to make each dress different in some way

(B) by saying that Weber has to sew very quickly in order to get the dresses done on time

(C) by describing how Weber uses the same pattern often because it is a familiar one

(D) by stating that Weber does most of her sewing by hand while sitting in her favorite place in the house

Part B: Which detail from the passage **best** supports your answer in Part A?

(A) "Each morning, the sound of a sewing machine fills Weber's farmhouse in the town of Bettendorf, Iowa."

(B) "When Weber is done at the sewing machine, she moves over to a comfortable chair."

(C) "She picks up the needle again to finish the dress she started that morning."

(D) "When she puts the finishing touches on a dress, she takes extra time to make each one special."

GO ON →

11 Read the sentence from the passage.

Now and then, Weber is able to see photographs of the young girls who have received her dresses.

Pick the word that provides the **best** clue to the meaning of the root word photo in the word photographs.

(A) chart

(B) drawing

(C) picture

(D) writing

12 The following question has two parts. First, answer part A. Then, answer part B.

Part A: Read the sentence from the passage.

Weber is sometimes referred to as the "Sewing Celebrity."

Which word is a synonym for celebrity?

(A) buddy

(B) circle

(C) star

(D) worker

Part B: Which sentence from the passage **best** supports your answer in part A?

(A) "She picks up the needle again to finish the dress she started that morning."

(B) "Weber learned about the group from her friend, Judy."

(C) "The women all decided to start making dresses."

(D) "The story of Lillian Weber's dedication has spread across the world as quickly as her dresses have."

GO ON →

13 This question has two parts. First, answer part A. Then, answer part B.

Part A: Which inference about the author's point of view is supported by the passage?

(A) The author admires what Lillian Weber does for others in need.

(B) The author wishes that all young people would be taught how to sew.

(C) The author thinks that Lillian Weber deserves to win many other awards.

(D) The author feels the woman who first heard of the project should be given credit.

Part B: Which sentence from the passage **best** supports your answer in part A?

(A) "She began stitching when she was only eight years old and has never stopped."

(B) "Seeing the happiness in the girls' smiles as they show off their new dresses is more than enough reward for this kind seamstress."

(C) "In turn, Judy had heard about it on a television show."

(D) "She won a local award as part of a TV series in Moline, Iowa, called 'Pay It Forward.'"

GO ON →

14 How does the author support the idea that Lillian Weber's dedication to making dresses is unusual or unique? Use details from the passage to support your answer.

_____

_____

_____

_____

_____

_____

Read the passages. Then answer the questions.

John Muir and the Fight for Hetch Hetchy

John Muir and his family came to the United States from Scotland when he was ten years old. He spent much of his life in Wisconsin, but he wanted to explore the West. At the age of 30, Muir arrived in San Francisco. The year was 1868. This was his first visit to California.

He traveled into the mountains known as the Sierra Nevada. The spectacular beauty of the wilderness greatly impressed Muir. He began to spend much of his time exploring and camping there.

Muir loved this land, especially a place known as the Yosemite Valley. In 1870, he began guiding tours in the area. The following year, he visited the Hetch Hetchy Valley. He was surprised to discover a second valley as beautiful as Yosemite! Swift rivers flowed through both valleys. Each was surrounded by towering cliffs. Both valleys were filled with waterfalls, flowering meadows, and ancient forests.

At this time, America was beginning to protect some of its wild places. Yellowstone became the first National Park in 1872. Muir supported the idea of public lands. He began writing and speaking about wilderness conservation. He wrote magazine articles describing the Sierra Nevada, Yosemite, and Hetch Hetchy. In fact, his words helped bring about the creation of Yosemite National Park in 1890.

A few years later, Muir met a young man named Gifford Pinchot. Pinchot wanted a career in forestry. Muir was delighted by the young man's interest in the science of managing and caring for forests. He encouraged Pinchot to spend time, not just studying forests, but actually living in them.

Muir became Pinchot's teacher and friend. The two journeyed together through the wilderness. Both men enjoyed living outdoors in all kinds of weather. They both wanted to protect America's forests. Muir and Pinchot agreed that the government should take control of forests and create rules for their use. Otherwise, people wanting to get rich in the mining or lumber industries might destroy America's forests forever.

GO ON →

Hetch Hetchy Reservoir

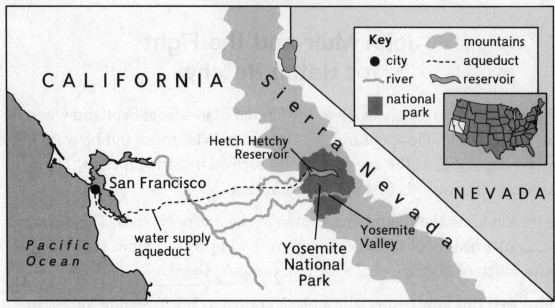

Muir and Pinchot did not agree on everything. Muir believed in the value of the beauty of nature. He believed that going to the wilderness was good for the body and spirit. He did not believe public lands should be used to make money.

Pinchot believed that it was important to let people profit from public lands. He argued that people could make good use of valuable natural resources, such as water, trees, and grass. He wanted to protect the natural world because it could be useful, with proper management, and not because it was beautiful.

In 1901, the city of San Francisco made a plan to put a dam in the Hetch Hetchy Valley. This dam would create a lake that would provide a dependable source of water for the growing city. Muir was horrified. There were other sources of water outside the park that could supply the city's water. He believed it would be wrong to destroy half of Yosemite National Park. Muir did all he could do to stop the project. He created pamphlets and wrote books. He took the President of the United States on a camping trip there.

Pinchot, on the other hand, agreed with the city of San Francisco. He believed the dam would provide the greatest good for the greatest number of people. His support was very important in the fight for the dam.

The battle over the dam went on for years. It destroyed the friendship between Muir and Pinchot. Finally, in 1913, San Francisco won the right to build the dam. Sadly, the Hetch Hetchy Valley disappeared forever under a great flood of water.

GO ON →

A Friend of Nature

Rachel Carson grew up on a farm in Pennsylvania. When Carson was a child, she and her dog, Candy, took long walks through the woods near the farm. They looked at the plants and listened to the sounds of birds and animals. Carson's mother encouraged her daughter's curiosity and love of nature. She helped Carson understand that people were a part of nature.

Her mother did a good job. Years later, Carson wanted to learn more about nature. She took classes in biology. She spent many hours walking through forests and fields studying plant and animal life. Before long, Carson knew she wanted to be a scientist.

Carson's work led her to the Massachusetts coast. She had never before seen the ocean. It was so different from the woods and fields of her Pennsylvania childhood. Carson spent many weeks near tide pools. Tide pools are rocky areas on the edge of the ocean that are filled with seawater. Here she saw unusual creatures she had never observed before. There were starfish in shades of bright red and light pink. Crabs of all sizes rushed to and fro like scurrying insects.

Carson decided to write a book about the sea. She wanted this book to help people discover the great beauty and dazzling variety of life sheltered by the ocean. She also wanted people to know that their lives on land depended on the sea. One of Carson's friends was an artist named Bob Hines. He drew many beautiful pictures for the book she wrote about the sea.

Throughout her life, Carson helped people understand that they should work with nature, not against it. Later, she spoke out against people hurting the environment. She fought against the use of dangerous chemicals that could hurt the environment.

GO ON →

One of her books made people aware of how important it is to protect the environment. In the book called *Silent Spring*, Carson warns that if we do not take better care of the environment, we could lose many animals. The title suggests that one day we might have a spring season in which no birds will be heard because they will have all died. At the time, some people accused Carson of making a mountain out of a molehill. Today, many people feel that this book started the movement to save the environment.

People did not always agree with Rachel Carson. But she fought for what she believed. In time, more and more people came to understand her point of view.

GO ON →

Answer these questions about "John Muir and the Fight for Hetch Hetchy."

15 Read the sentence from the passage.

He wanted to protect the natural world because it could be useful, with proper <u>management</u>, and not because it was beautiful.

Manage can mean "to direct." What does <u>management</u> mean in the sentence above?

(A) change

(B) control

(C) thought

(D) training

16 Why does the author compare the views of Muir and Pinchot?

(A) to show the arguments for and against the Hetch Hetchy dam

(B) to show that Californians needed water from the dam to drink

(C) to show how building the dam would harm the environment

(D) to show the reasons the dam was a good idea and why people wanted it

17 What reasons does the author give for Muir's disapproval of the plans to build a dam in the Hetch Hetchy Valley? Use details from the passage to support your answer.

_____

_____

_____

_____

_____

_____

GO ON →

Answer these questions about "A Friend of Nature."

18 Read the sentences from "A Friend of Nature."

Carson's work led her to the Massachusetts coast. She had never before seen the <u>ocean</u>. It was so different from the woods and fields of her Pennsylvania childhood.

Which word helps you understand the meaning of <u>ocean</u>?

(A) work

(B) coast

(C) fields

(D) childhood

19 Why does the author **most likely** include information about Carson's childhood in the passage? Pick **all** that apply.

(A) to prove that stories about children are entertaining

(B) to tell how childhood can influence a person's career

(C) to show that biographies need to include time in childhood

(D) to reflect the impact of Carson's mother on Carson's choices

(E) to make a point about how Carson's mother believed children should be raised

(F) to show that children should study hard in school so they can pursue their passions

(G) to show Carson's willingness to study a subject different from what she had grown up with

GO ON →

20 Why does the author consider Carson to be "a friend of nature"? Use details from the passage to support your answer.

_____

_____

_____

_____

_____

_____

Now answer this question about "John Muir and the Fight for Hetch Hetchy" and "A Friend of Nature."

21 Think about how the authors of "John Muir and the Fight for Hetch Hetchy" and "A Friend of Nature" describe Muir and Carson fighting for what they believed. To what extent do the authors suggest that Muir and Carson succeeded in their fights? Use details from both passages to support your answer.

_____

_____

_____

_____

_____

_____

_____

_____

_____

_____

_____

GO ON →

The passage below needs revision. Read the passage. Then answer the questions.

I want to express a big thank-you to everyone who ___(1)___ to the Book Fair last week. The money we earned will buy at least 20 new books for the school library. The Book Fair ___(2)___ a huge success!

Are you ready for some more action? Kayeesha, Noah, and I ___(3)___ the Fall Harvest Festival. The festival will be on November 15. It ___(4)___ a great success in the past. But we'll need a lot of volunteers.

GO ON →

22 Which answer should go in blank (1)?

   (A) came

   (B) comes

   (C) was coming

23 Which answer should go in blank (2)?

   (A) is

   (B) was

   (C) will be

24 Which answer should go in blank (3)?

   (A) plan

   (B) are planning

   (C) am planning

25 Which answer should go in blank (4)?

   (A) will be

   (B) been

   (C) has been

GO ON →

The passage below needs revision. Read the passage. Then answer the questions.

Have you ever ____(1)____ a news announcement? Can you draw? ____(2)____ you good at making posters? If so, we ____(3)____ your talent on the Publicity Team.

Last year, a group of fourth graders ____(4)____ a wonderful puppet show. They performed "The Very Hungry Caterpillar" and ____(5)____ us all a good laugh. We are hoping that some talented actors will plan a performance for this year's festival.

Of course, yummy food is the best part of the Harvest Festival. The pies and spiced cider always ____(6)____ so good! We'll need some great cooks. Please join us as a volunteer and make this year's Fall Harvest Festival the best ever.

GO ON →

26 Which answer should go in blank (1)?

Ⓐ write

Ⓑ wrote

Ⓒ written

27 Which answer should go in blank (2)?

Ⓐ Are

Ⓑ Am

Ⓒ Is

28 Which answer should go in blank (3)?

Ⓐ use

Ⓑ can use

Ⓒ have used

29 Which answer should go in blank (4)?

Ⓐ presented

Ⓑ are presenting

Ⓒ will present

30 Which answer should go in blank (5)?

Ⓐ give

Ⓑ gave

Ⓒ gived

31 Which answer should go in blank (6)?

Ⓐ tasting

Ⓑ tastes

Ⓒ taste

Opinion Performance Task

Task:

Your class is creating an online newsletter about how people can make a difference in the world. For your part of the newsletter, you will write an opinion paper about the best ways individuals and companies can help others. Your opinion will be read by other students, teachers, parents, and other people who read the school's online newsletter.

After you have reviewed these sources, you will answer some questions about them. Briefly scan the sources and three questions that follow. Then, go back and read the sources carefully to gain the information you will need to answer the questions and write an opinion paper for class.

In Part 2, you will write your opinion paper using information from the two sources.

Directions for Part 1

You will now look at the two sources. You can look at either of the sources as often as you like.

Research Questions:

After reviewing the research sources, use the rest of the time in Part 1 to answer three questions about them. Your answers to these questions will be scored. Also, your answers will help you think about the information you have read and viewed, which should help you write your opinion paper.

You may take notes on scratch paper and refer back to your scratch paper to review your notes when you think it would be helpful.

Your written notes will be available to you in Part 1 and Part 2 of the performance task.

GO ON →

Source #1: The Pavement Bookworm

When Philani Dladla walks down the sidewalks of Johannesburg, a city in South Africa, he grabs people's attention. Dressed in a baseball hat, brightly striped dress shirt, and strands of colorful beads, he is like a moving rainbow. What really makes Dladla stand out, however, is the stack of books he is carrying around with him. Those books, and what he does with them, have earned him the nickname "Pavement Bookworm."

Sure, Dladla loves to read. He says it changed his life. His first book was a gift when he was eight years old. He taught himself to read it in English. He read it over and over. As he grew up, the young man struggled with many problems. He began reading self-help books to find some answers and guidance. He discovered that reading helped him become a happier, more knowledgeable person. That passion for books is now what drives him. He spends every day out on the city sidewalks sharing books with anyone who stops by to look. He finds a busy intersection and sits down. Next, he opens a book, starts to read, and waits for the first person to stop and ask a question.

Dladla is always happy to describe a plot or share a favorite title. He also enjoys having an in-depth discussion about authors, ideas, and publishers. Adults often give Dladla a donation for the book they end up taking along with them. Children, however, are allowed to pick any book he has for free. The Pavement Bookworm loves knowing that he is making a difference in their lives by handing them a book. He believes that kids need to read so they can learn and make wiser decisions as they grow, and so they can have a better chance of getting hired in the future. Dladla's philosophy is simple. He believes that if you have inspired a single person, you have changed the world.

Philani Dladla's story was first shared with the world in late November 2013. A South African filmmaker named Tebogo Malope spotted Dladla walking along the city streets. He saw him sit down on a bench, put down his pile of books, and start reading. Within a few minutes, people were stopping by to chat.

GO ON →

Malope recorded a video interview with the 25-year-old reader. He posted it online. It did not take long for the story to spread across the globe. Soon, Dladla was being interviewed on a number of radio programs and in magazine articles. News spread quickly through Johannesburg also. Now the bookworm has become a local celebrity. People stop him every day to ask about books. They ask him what they should ready next. Authors have even traveled to visit Dladla. They give him copies of their books to hand out or give away.

Today, Dladla's life is busy with sharing books and organizing reading clubs for young people. The clubs have members from young kids through college students. He hands out books to each one. They read the book. Then, they get together to discuss the ideas in what they have read. To make sure that Dladla does not run out of books to sell and give away to others, Malope has been collecting book donations for the Pavement Bookworm. He calls the young man "an amazing ambassador for young people." He wants to do all he can to help a young man whose passion for the written word keeps him going—and sharing.

Source #2: From Box to Backpack

Many people know that cardboard boxes are recyclable and generally helpful to have around. They can be used to mail packages, help a person move, or hold anything from a load of books to a set of dishes. However, it took a nonprofit organization called Aarambh in New Bombay, India, to find out just how amazingly helpful these recycled boxes can be.

Aarambh is based in New Bombay. Since its start in 1996, the group has focused on providing educational skills and assistance to children and women throughout India. "Aarambh" is a word that means "beginnings." The organization's main goal is to move "towards a brighter future."

The staff at Aarambh knew that most of the students in Indian schools did not have chairs and desks to sit at or backpacks to carry their books and other supplies. Instead, students sat on the floor, their notebooks spread out in front of them. Naturally, this made it difficult to write clearly and sit comfortably. In addition, students had to carry their school materials home

GO ON →

in their arms, or inside fragile plastic shopping bags, which were constantly tearing and falling apart.

At Aarambh, the workers wanted to improve the situation for the students. The staff developed the Help Desk. It is easily portable. The desks are made out of nothing but recycled cardboard boxes. When folded one direction, the boxes provide a sturdy desk with an angled surface for writing and reading. At the end of the day, students can unfold their desks and turn them into carriers to wear on their backs. Flat and rectangular, the carriers look like briefcases. They have a handle that makes it possible to carry them in one hand, or they can also slide onto students' backs.

Aarambh uses the cardboard it gathers from local recycling centers, offices and businesses. Using free materials helps to reduce the cost of manufacturing the desks. In fact, each eco-friendly Help Desk costs less than 20 cents to make.

The process is fairly simple. First, workers carefully trace the outline of the Help Desk onto the flattened out cardboard. Next, they use a laser to cut the sheets of cardboard. Finally, they begin to fold this way and that. Suddenly a desk appears, as if by magic.

The Aarambh organization distributed the Help Desks to schools throughout Maharashtra, a state in India's western region. Not too surprisingly, the desks were a big hit with the students. They quickly learned how to fold and unfold the boxes. They had fun switching them from desks to backpacks and back again. Having a surface to write on has made reading, writing, and doing school work far more comfortable. It lessens eye strain and back strain. It also improves overall posture. Best of all, it makes learning easier for the students and encourages them to stay in school.

GO ON →

Name: _____ Date: _____

 Both of these sources provide information on how people have made a difference in the world by making it easier for others to learn and further their education. Draw a line from each source to choose **one** sentence in the list from Source #1 and **one** sentence in the list from Source #2 that best support this idea.

Source #1

"Those books, and what he does with them, have earned him the nickname 'Pavement Bookworm.'"

Source #2

"Best of all, it makes learning easier for the students and encourages them to stay in school."

"He began reading self-help books to find some answers and guidance."

"Many people know that cardboard boxes are recyclable, and generally helpful to have around."

"He believes that kids need to read so they can think and make wiser decisions as they grow, and have a better chance of getting hired in the future."

"At the end of the day, students can unfold their desks and turn them into carriers to wear on their backs."

GO ON →

Name: _____ Date: _____

2 Both "The Pavement Bookworm" and "From Box to Backpack" discuss how to make a difference in the world. What does "The Pavement Bookworm" explain about helping people that "From Box to Backpack" does not? Explain why that information is helpful for the reader. Give **two** details or examples from "The Pavement Bookworm" to support your explanation.

_____

_____

_____

_____

3 "From Box to Backpack" includes information about helping others. Explain how this information would be helpful if it were added to "The Pavement Bookworm." Give **two** details or examples from "From Box to Backpack" to support your explanation.

_____

_____

_____

_____

_____

GO ON →

Directions for Part 2

You will now review your notes and sources, and plan, draft, revise, and edit your writing. You may use your notes and go back to the sources. Now read your assignment and the information about how your writing will be scored; then begin your work.

Your Assignment:

Your teacher has asked everyone in the class to write an opinion paper that will be used in the school's online newsletter. You are going to write an opinion paper about whether a person can make a bigger and/or better difference in a community if they are working alone or with a group. Your paper will be read by other students, teachers, and parents.

Using both "The Pavement Bookworm" and "From Box to Backpack," develop an opinion about the most effective ways to make a difference in the community. Choose the most important information from both sources to support your opinion. Then, write an opinion paper several paragraphs long. Clearly organize your paper and support your opinion with details from the sources. Use your own words except when quoting directly from the sources. Be sure to give the source title or number when using details from the sources.

REMEMBER: A well-written opinion paper

- has a clear main idea.
- is well-organized and stays on the topic.
- has an introduction and conclusion.
- uses transitions.
- uses details from the sources to support your opinion.
- puts the information from the sources in your own words, except when using direct quotations from the sources.
- gives the title or number of the source for the details or facts you included.
- develops ideas clearly.
- uses clear language.
- follows rules of writing (spelling, punctuation, and grammar usage).

Now begin work on your opinion paper. Manage your time carefully so that you can plan, write, revise, and edit the final draft of your opinion paper. Write your response on a separate sheet of paper.

STOP

Question	Correct Answer	Content Focus	CCSS	Complexity
1A	C	Greek Roots	L.4.4b	DOK 2
1B	B	Greek Roots/Text Evidence	L.4.4b/ RL.4.1	DOK 2
2A	D	Context Clues: Synonyms	L.4.5c	DOK 2
2B	D	Context Clues: Synonyms/Text Evidence	L.4.5c/ RL.4.1	DOK 2
3A	D	Point of View	RL.4.6	DOK 2
3B	C	Point of View/Text Evidence	RL.4.6/ RL.4.1	DOK 2
4A	B	Point of View	RL.4.6	DOK 3
4B	C	Point of View/Text Evidence	RL.4.6/ RL.4.1	DOK 3
5	see below	Point of View	RL.4.6	DOK 2
6	B	Context Clues: Definitions and Restatements	L.4.4a	DOK 2
7	see below	Point of View	RL.4.6	DOK 3
8A	C	Context Clues: Paragraph Clues	L.4.4a	DOK 2
8B	A	Context Clues: Paragraph Clues/ Text Evidence	L.4.4a/ RI.4.1	DOK 2
9	see below	Author's Point of View	RI.4.8	DOK 2
10A	A	Author's Point of View	RI.4.8	DOK 2
10B	D	Author's Point of View/Text Evidence	RI.4.8/ RI.4.1	DOK 2
11	C	Greek Roots	L.4.4b	DOK 2
12A	C	Context Clues: Synonyms	L.4.5c	DOK 2
12B	D	Context Clues: Synonyms/Text Evidence	L.4.5c/ RI.4.1	DOK 2
13A	A	Author's Point of View	RI.4.8	DOK 3
13B	B	Author's Point of View/Text Evidence	RI.4.8/ RI.4.1	DOK 3
14	see below	Author's Point of View	RI.4.8	DOK 3
15	B	Latin and Greek Suffixes	L.4.4b	DOK 2
16	A	Author's Point of View	RI.4.8	DOK 3
17	see below	Author's Point of View	RI.4.8	DOK 3

Question	Correct Answer	Content Focus	CCSS	Complexity
18	B	Context Clues: Definitions and Restatements	L.4.4a	DOK 2
19	B, D, G	Author's Point of View	RI.4.8	DOK 3
20	see below	Author's Point of View	RI.4.8	DOK 3
21	see below	Compare Across Texts	W.4.9b	DOK 4
22	A	Action Verbs	L.3.1d	DOK 1
23	B	Linking Verbs	L.4.1	DOK 1
24	B	Verb Tenses	L.4.1b	DOK 1
25	C	Main and Helping Verbs	L.4.1	DOK 1
26	C	Irregular Verbs	L.3.1d	DOK 1
27	A	Linking Verbs	L.3.1f	DOK 1
28	B	Main and Helping Verbs	L.4.1	DOK 1
29	A	Action Verbs	L.3.1d	DOK 1
30	B	Irregular Verbs	L.3.1d	DOK 1
31	C	Types of Pronouns	L.3.1a	DOK 1

Comprehension: Selected Response 3A, 3B, 4A, 4B, 9, 12A, 12B, 13A, 13B, 16, 19	/14	%
Comprehension: Constructed Response 5, 7, 14, 17, 20, 21	/14	%
Vocabulary 1A, 1B, 2A, 2B, 6, 8A, 8B, 10, 11, 15, 18	/16	%
English Language Conventions 22–31	/10	%
Total Unit Assessment Score	/54	%

5 Students should draw lines to match the following:
- Cally: making signs
- Max: researching the topic

7 **2-point response:** The Critter Crossing project is a great project for Iman because she is really interested in animals. She has lots of pets at home and is accused by Theo of thinking of animals all the time.

9 Students should draw lines to match the following:
- reason to include Weber's age: to highlight her energy and dedication to helping others
- reason to include Weber's age: to emphasize how unusual it is for a person her age to be this active
- reason to include Weber's age: to show how she is different from the typical seamstress

14 **2-point response:** The author supports the idea that Lillian Weber's dedication is unusual by describing how she is almost 100 years old and has been sewing almost every day since she was eight years old, and how she makes a new dress every day. She also has an unusual goal of making 1,000 dresses for the project "Little Dresses for Africa" by the time she turns 100.

17 **2-point response:** John Muir's dedication to protecting the wilderness in the United States was demonstrated in the work he did by writing about the Sierra Nevada Mountains, Yosemite, and Hetch Hetchy, and in how he helped create Yosemite National Park in 1890. Muir did not agree with or approve of Gifford Pinchot's efforts to allow people to profit off public lands, so he wrote pamphlets and books about this and even took the President of the United States on a camping trip to the Yosemite area.

20 **2-point response:** Rachel Carson wrote a book about the sea because she wanted people to know that their lives depended on the health of the sea and that they could hurt the environment by their actions. Later she wrote a book called *Silent Spring* that warns about how many animals could die if we aren't careful to protect the environment.

21 **4-point response:** The authors describe how Rachel Carson and John Muir both fought to protect the environment and both had some success. John Muir fought for wilderness conservation. When people began to think about protecting public lands in America, Muir supported this idea. He wrote articles describing wilderness areas. The author describes some of Muir's successes, such as when he helped in establishing the creation of Yosemite National Park in 1890. However, the author also describes how Muir tried but failed to prevent the building of the dam in Hetch Hetchy. Hetch Hetchy Valley no longer exists for people to see because it is under water. But without Muir's help, something like this could have happened to the rest of Yosemite too.

Rachel Carson also fought to protect the environment. She wrote about the importance of keeping the oceans clean and about public awareness. The author says that many people today feel that one of her books, *Silent Spring*, started the movement to save the environment by warning people that all the animals could die if we don't protect them. This suggests that Carson had a lot of success in changing the world. However, the author also notes that some people at the time accused Carson of "making a mountain out of a molehill," which suggests that she failed to make everyone listen to her. She wasn't able to fix all the problems that animals face. Neither Muir nor Carson achieved everything they hoped to, but they both made a difference.

Answer Key

Name: _____

Opinion Performance Task				
Question	**Answer**	**CCSS**	**Complexity**	**Score**
1	see below	RI.4.1, RI.4.2, RI.4.3, RI.4.7, RI.4.8, RI.4.9 W.4.1a-d, W.4.4, W.4.7 L.4.1, L.4.2	DOK 3	/1
2	see below		DOK 3	/2
3	see below		DOK 3	/2
Opinion Paper	see below		DOK 4	/4 [P/O] /4 [E/E] /2 [C]
Total Score				**/15**

1 Students should draw lines to match the following statements:
  • Source #1: "He believes that kids need to read so they can think and make wiser decisions as they grow, and have a better chance of getting hired in the future."
  • Source #2: "Best of all, it makes learning easier for the students and encourages them to stay in school."

2 **2-point response:** "The Pavement Bookworm" shows how you can make a difference all by yourself, rather than having to be part of a company or organization. It focuses on the difference an individual can make within the community. It also points out that how Dladla helps people he comes into contact with face to face, and of all ages, rather than specific ages and groups. That is inspiring for others who would like to make differences but are not sure how to do so.

3 **2-point response:** "From Box to Backpack" includes information on how to help a greater number of people at a time, rather than the individual who may or may not stop by to chat. In addition, it shows how the idea can be shared with others in order to have a greater impact on the world. This information would be great if added to "The Pavement Bookworm" as it would show how Dladla's idea could ripple out and affect more people.

10-point anchor paper: I believe that Philani Dladla is performing an excellent community service by handing out and selling books to people. However, I feel that the employees at Aarambh are making a bigger impact on their community.

Instead of reaching the people who may stop by and chat, as with Dladla, the Indian company is making products that are being sent out to much larger groups of people. They are not waiting for someone to approach them for help or suggestions, as with the Pavement Bookworm, but are instead producing portable desks and sending them to classrooms. In addition, the work they do to make these cardboard desks can be shared with others and spread out across the world to wherever the desks may help.

Aarambh is not only helping get people interested in reading but actually helping students study all the different subjects they learn in school. It is improving students' lives by providing cardboard desks so they can write comfortably. The desks are eco-friendly, cost less than 20 cents each to make, and can be easily carried as a backpack. Students like them and stay in school longer because the desks relieve eye strain and back strain. So Aarambh is living up to its name, which means "beginnings," and its goal of moving "towards a brighter future."

Based on what I learned here, it is my opinion that working with a group of people is the most effective way to make a difference in the world. Since you have more money, help, and materials, you can reach more people and cause a bigger ripple to spread across the world.

Read the passage. Then answer the questions.

The Great Road Race

Reporter:

A crowd of spectators is gathering here.

They're ready to watch, and they're eager to cheer,

For today is the day of a special road race.

Here come the two runners who'll try for first place.

These two competitors make a strange pair—

A slow, plodding Tortoise and a fast, frisky Hare.

In his colorful outfit, Hare is looking the part.

Wearing only his shell, Tortoise plods toward the start.

Tortoise:

I'll just keep going; it's all I can do.

I know I am slow, but I'm steady, too.

Hare:

Oh, ho—look at me!

I'm as fast as can be!

Today I'm sure to shine,

Victory will be mine.

Mouse:

I'm rooting for Hare,

who is flashy and bright.

I'm betting he'll win,

and I'm sure I'll be right.

I like Tortoise, too—

he's a nice enough guy,

but he can't win the race,

even though he will try.

GO ON →

Reporter:

With a "ready, set, go!" the race has begun.
Hare hops off in a flash—just look at him run!
As everyone knows, Hare is charming and fast,
But his mind often wanders, so his speed may not last.

Tortoise starts slowly; step by step he takes off.
He's falling behind, so some people may scoff.
But he sticks to a task, on that you can depend,
His patience may help him to win in the end.

Hare:

Oh, ho—look at me!
I'm as fast as can be!
Today I'm sure to shine,
Victory will be mine.

For me this race will be over in a snap;
I'd still win even if I took a nap.
I can't even see him, he's so far behind.
I'll stop for a snack—the spectators won't mind.

Mmm, look at those carrots, and look at those peas!
I'll eat from this garden as long as I please,
and after I've eaten, I'll lie down to rest.
When I'm feeling tired, I can't run my best.

Reporter:

Hare has fallen asleep, which may not be smart.
When you don't pay attention, your plan falls apart.
And here comes the Tortoise! He's not flashy or fast,
but he seems unwilling to end this race last.

Tortoise:

Oh, me, oh, my, I've traveled a mile,
and I see that Hare has paused for a while.
I'll just keep going; it's all I can do.
I know I'm slow, but I'm steady, too.

GO ON →

Hare:

I've enjoyed a nice rest,
but I'd better get going.
Tortoise might have gone by
without my knowing.

Oh, ho—look at me!
I'm as fast as can be!
Today I'm sure to shine,
Victory will be mine.

Reporter:

Now the great road race is nearing its end.
Here comes the Hare, speeding 'round the bend,
but Tortoise has just stepped over the line—
he got there first! It's his turn to shine!

Mouse:

Wow! Look at Tortoise!
His chances seemed zero,
but he's won the race,
so now he's my hero!

Reporter:

Well, that's it, folks; the race is done.
Hare was favored, but Tortoise won.
Fast and flashy is not always the way;
Sometimes slow and steady wins the day.

GO ON →

1 The following question has two parts. First, answer part A. Then, answer part B.

Part A: Read the stanza from the passage.

Mouse:

I'm <u>rooting</u> for Hare,
who is flashy and bright.
I'm betting he'll win,
and I'm sure I'll be right.

What does the word <u>rooting</u> mean as it is used in the passage?

(A) checking

(B) cheering

(C) waiting

(D) watching

Part B: Which detail from the passage **best** supports your answer in part A?

(A) ". . . betting he'll win . . ."

(B) ". . . sure I'll be right . . ."

(C) ". . . nice enough guy . . ."

(D) ". . . he will try . . ."

GO ON →

2 This question has two parts. First, answer part A. Then, answer part B.

Part A: Read the lines from the passage.

For me this race will be <u>over in a snap</u>;
I'd still win even if I took a nap.
I can't even see him, he's so far behind.
I'll stop for a snack—the spectators won't mind.

What does the poet's use of the phrase "over in a snap" help the reader understand about Hare?

(A) Hare feels that the race will be fun.

(B) Hare feels that the race will be loud.

(C) Hare feels that the race will be quick.

(D) Hare feels that the race will be tiring.

Part B: Which detail from the passage **best** supports your answer in part A?

(A) "I'm as fast as can be!"

(B) "I'd still win even if I took a nap."

(C) "I can't even see him, he's so far behind."

(D) "I'll stop for a snack—the spectators won't mind."

GO ON →

3 Which words from the passage have **almost** the same meaning as plodding? Pick **two** choices.

(A) bright

(B) frisky

(C) fast

(D) charming

(E) steady

(F) slow

(G) unwilling

4 The poet uses one element that is the **same** in the stanzas spoken by Hare. Which element used in these stanzas is the **same**?

(A) the use of a dash

(B) the use of repetition

(C) the lengths of the lines

(D) the number of rhyming words

GO ON →

5 The following question has two parts. First, answer part A. Then, answer part B.

Part A: Which character in the passage speaks using the third-person point of view?

Ⓐ Hare

Ⓑ Mouse

Ⓒ Reporter

Ⓓ Tortoise

Part B: Which line from the passage **best** supports your answer in part A?

Ⓐ "They're ready to watch, and they're eager to cheer, . . ."

Ⓑ "I'll just keep going; it's all I can do."

Ⓒ "Oh, ho—look at me!"

Ⓓ "I'm betting he'll win, . . ."

GO ON →

6 The following question has two parts. First, answer part A. Then, answer part B.

Part A: Which sentence **best** tells the theme of the passage?

(A) Winners do not stop trying.

(B) It is important to learn from mistakes.

(C) Do not put all your eggs in one basket.

(D) It is foolish to bite off more than you can chew.

Part B: Which sentence from the passage **best** supports your answer in part A?

(A) "I'll just keep going; it's all I can do."

(B) "I'd still win even if I took a nap."

(C) "I'll eat from this garden as long as I please . . ."

(D) "Oh, me, oh, my, I've traveled a mile . . ."

7 What is the **most likely** reason the poet had two speakers in the poem repeat certain lines? What do the repeated lines tell you about the personalities of the speakers? Use information from the passage to support your answer.

_____

_____

_____

_____

_____

GO ON →

Read the passage. Then answer the questions.

No Escape from Sherlock Holmes

As 1893 drew to a close, the author admitted he had finally had enough. He was weary of writing about the same characters over and over again. He was tired of meeting deadlines. Since he had invented his characters, he knew he could also bring them to a dramatic end whenever he wanted. With the touch of his pen, Arthur Conan Doyle decided to write his last story about the famous detective, Sherlock Holmes.

The End of Sherlock

In the story "The Final Problem," Sherlock Holmes figured out the last clue, solved the last mystery, and fought his old enemy, Professor Moriarty, for the last time. This time, however, the clever man did not win. Instead he fell over the side of a Swiss waterfall with his enemy. At last, Holmes was gone. Doyle could get back to the style of writing he liked more, historical fiction.

While Doyle may have been delighted to move on, his fans were anything but happy. In fact, they were furious! For years, mysteries about Sherlock Holmes and his faithful sidekick, Dr. John Watson, had been printed in England's The Strand Magazine. Each issue contained another story. Readers loved discovering the new adventures of Holmes and Watson each month. Thousands of people subscribed to the magazine to read the newest Sherlock adventure as soon as possible. In 1890, the second Sherlock novel penned by Doyle, *The Sign of the Four*, thrilled readers. Story after story followed with a new adventure every few months. By 1893, everyone was talking about Holmes and Watson. Libraries lost track of the number of readers coming to get copies of the detective tales. Printing presses struggled to keep up with the demand.

Against the Tide of Public Opinion

Abruptly, the public's favorite crime-fighting duo was gone. Angry readers stood outside the offices of The Strand in protest. Some wore black arm bands as a symbol of their sadness. Others wrote letters to Doyle pleading with him to bring Sherlock back. Hundreds of people cancelled their subscriptions to The Strand. The public outcry came to be known as "the dreadful event."

GO ON →

The protest by Doyle's fans was not enough to get him to change his mind. He was firm about leaving Holmes and Watson behind. He was determined to focus his writing on historical events. He wanted to be thought of as a serious writer, not a popular one. Doyle was stubborn, and he did not give in when his friends, and even his mother, begged him to return to the tales of Sherlock Holmes.

Triumphant Return

Finally, however, in 1902, an American publisher made Doyle an offer he could not refuse. He offered the author $5,000 to bring back the beloved detective for one single story. That was an incredible amount of money at the time (it would be worth approximately $135,000 today). Doyle could not resist such a remarkable offer. He wrote the novel *The Hound of the Baskervilles*. He kept writing, too. By the time he finally finished writing about Sherlock Holmes, he had written 56 stories and four novels about Holmes and Watson.

Doyle passed away in 1930. Even at the end, he still was not pleased with his fame as the inventor of one of literature's most well-known detectives. Many people have wondered what the author would have thought if he had known how he would be viewed over time. Over a century later, his characters and their incredible mystery-solving skills are still popular. In fact, they have been featured in countless short stories, novels, movies, and even television shows. Perhaps he would have been pleased that instead of simply writing about history, his imagination and talent ended up becoming a part of literary history.

GO ON →

8 Read the sentences from the passage.

While Doyle may have been delighted to move on, his fans were anything but happy. In fact, they were <u>furious</u>!

Which words are synonyms of <u>furious</u>? Pick **two** choices.

(A) angry

(B) mad

(C) noisy

(D) tired

(E) frightened

9 Read the sentence from the passage.

<u>Abruptly</u>, the public's favorite crime-fighting duo was gone.

What does the Latin root *rupt* mean in the word <u>abruptly</u>?

(A) break

(B) close

(C) join

(D) mend

GO ON →

10 The following question has two parts. First, answer part A. Then, answer part B.

Part A: Which is **most likely** the reason that Arthur Conan Doyle stopped writing about Sherlock Holmes?

(A) Doyle was hoping to write less frequently.

(B) Doyle wanted to write about other detectives.

(C) Doyle wanted to write a different type of fiction.

(D) Doyle was unhappy about the fame he had achieved.

Part B: Which sentence from the passage **best** supports your answer in part A?

(A) "He was weary of writing about the same characters over and over again."

(B) "He was tired of meeting deadlines."

(C) "Doyle could get back to the style of writing he liked more, historical fiction."

(D) "Even at the end, he still was not pleased with his fame as the inventor of one of literature's most well-known detectives."

11 Why did the author **most likely** use the words "Triumphant Return" in boldfaced type in the passage? Pick **all** that apply.

(A) The author wants to use these words as a heading for the next section.

(B) The author wants to explain why Doyle stopped writing about Sherlock Holmes.

(C) The author wants to tell the reader about why a different style of writing is better.

(D) The author wants to show the reader Doyle's indecision about writing about Sherlock Holmes.

(E) The author wants to give the reader a clue about what is coming next for Doyle and Sherlock Holmes.

(F) The author wants to introduce the American publisher who offered Doyle a large amount of money to bring Sherlock Holmes back to the readers.

GO ON →

12 The following question has two parts. First, answer part A. Then, answer part B.

Part A: Read the sentence from the passage.

Thousands of people <u>subscribed to</u> the magazine to read the newest Sherlock adventure as soon as possible.

Which **best** matches the meaning of "subscribed to"?

(A) paid extra money for

(B) bought their friends copies of

(C) rushed to the library to look for

(D) signed up to get future issues of

Part B: Which sentence from the passage **best** supports your answer in part A?

(A) Readers loved discovering the new adventures of Holmes and Watson each month.

(B) Libraries lost track of the number of readers coming to get copies of the detective tales.

(C) Printing presses struggled to keep up with the demand.

(D) Doyle could not resist such a remarkable offer.

13 Which events **most likely** led to the American publisher offering Arthur Conan Doyle money to write about Sherlock Holmes again? Number the **three** events in the order they occurred.

_____ Arthur Conan Doyle wrote stories that have been turned into movies.

_____ Arthur Conan Doyle wrote stories that became very popular for a magazine.

_____ Arthur Conan Doyle wanted to write about something that would be read by more people.

_____ Arthur Conan Doyle decided to write about what interested him most.

_____ Arthur Conan Doyle wrote more short stories than novels.

_____ Arthur Conan Doyle was begged to continue writing the stories that made him famous.

14 What is the **most likely** reason Arthur Conan Doyle not only changed his mind about writing about Sherlock Holmes but also continued writing about him until his death in 1930?

_____

_____

_____

_____

_____

GO ON →

Read the passages. Then answer the questions.

Bessie Coleman and Me

The first time I was in a school play, I felt extremely uneasy. I was scared that I would make a mistake and people would laugh at me. In the weeks before opening night, I spent a lot of time around the house nervously going over my lines. I had a great time rehearsing with the other cast members, but when I got home, the fear set in. I had a hard time concentrating on my homework, and I was so nervous that I could barely eat dinner sometimes.

I didn't think anyone noticed what was happening, but apparently my brother Jeremy did. Even though we don't always have much in common, I have to admit that he can be pretty smart sometimes.

One night after dinner, Jeremy saw me in the den staring blankly at my math book. "What are you doing, Emily?" he asked. "It looks like you are sleeping sitting up."

"I'm studying," I answered, "so please leave me alone!"

I must have needed to confide in someone, though, because he ended up getting me to tell him what was going on. I told Jeremy the whole story—the play, my nerves, everything.

GO ON →

He said, "I just read an inspiring book about Bessie Coleman, and I think you should read it. She was the first female African-American pilot in the country. She had many incredible problems to overcome. Her family was poor, and she could not go to school full-time. When she was in her early twenties, the only thing Bessie wanted to do was to fly a plane. However, it was extremely difficult for African Americans to become pilots. She worked hard, though, and later became a pilot. I think you should read the book."

I was curious, so I took the book and read it right then. Jeremy was right. Bessie Coleman was an incredibly interesting person. Even though she wasn't able to go to school all the time, when she was young, she took books out of the library and studied them on her own. When she was older, she read all she could about flying. She desperately wanted to be a pilot.

Flight schools in America would not take Bessie because she was an African American and a woman, but this did not stop her. She was so determined to go to flight school that she used all her savings from working two jobs, studied French on her own, and left for flight school in 1920. She attended flight school in France, learned to fly, and successfully reached her goal of receiving her pilot's license. She returned to America and began performing in air shows.

After I read this story, I was so inspired! I knew that if Bessie could overcome that many obstacles to become a pilot, and perform in air shows in front of all those people, I didn't need to be afraid of acting in a school play!

The opening night of the play turned out to be fun and not scary at all. I felt a few butterflies in my stomach, but I thought of Bessie flying bravely in the sky, and my courage grew.

Many people paid me compliments on my performance, including my brother Jeremy. After he congratulated me, I said these two little words to my big brother: "Thank you." And I secretly thanked Bessie Coleman too.

GO ON →

Bessie Coleman

Bessie Coleman was the first female African-American pilot, and experts believe that she was the third African American to receive a pilot's license. There were few ways to earn a living as a pilot in those days. Bessie, however, was successful in building a career as a famous barnstormer. She traveled from town to town performing dangerous stunts in the air.

Bessie Coleman, 1892–1926

High Hopes

Bessie was born in Atlanta, Texas, in the early 1890s. She had twelve brothers and sisters. Bessie's family was poor, so as Bessie grew older, she helped tend the house and take care of the younger children. Bessie was excited about school and loved to learn, and she was especially good at math. Even though she loved school, she often had to leave school to work to help the family.

Bessie went to an industrial college for a short period of time after finishing eighth grade. At that time, flying was a new and exciting adventure. Bessie read about the Wright Brothers and their historic flight at Kitty Hawk in 1903. She also read about Harriet Quimby, a female aviator. Bessie was surprised to learn that a woman could be a pilot, and she started to think about flying herself.

In 1915, Bessie moved to Chicago to live with family. She found work, saved her money, and set out to learn to fly. She soon discovered that this could never happen in the United States. No flying school would take an African American, and especially a woman, as a student. If she was going to learn to fly, she would have to move to France where schools were more accepting of women and African Americans.

GO ON →

Flying High

In 1920, Bessie arrived in France and began flying lessons. She learned how to take off and land, how to bank turns, and how to loop-the-loop. After nearly a year of lessons, Bessie became the first female African American to ever earn a pilot's license.

When Bessie arrived home in the United States, she found herself surrounded by reporters. An African-American pilot was big news! She told them her dream was to open a flying school that was open to everyone.

Bessie knew her dream would cost a lot. To earn money she began performing in air shows, which were very dangerous. Audiences at these shows wanted to see thrilling, perilous stunts. However, Bessie was fearless.

Queen Bess

Bessie performed all kinds of stunts. Often her final stunt was the most exciting. She would fly high up into the sky. Then she turned straight down, pulling out of the dive at the very last moment. Sometimes she flew right over the audience's heads! Bessie's popularity grew, and she became a local hero. She was even nicknamed "Queen Bess." Bessie soon began performing all around the country.

On April 30, 1926, Bessie was in Florida preparing for an upcoming air show. She had planned to parachute jump out of the plane for her last exciting stunt. She and her mechanic William Wills took the plane up to practice the stunt with William in the pilot's seat. During the practice, the plane became unstable and flipped over. Bessie was thrown from the plane before it crashed. Both Bessie and William were killed.

Today, Bessie's spirit of courage and determination still inspires people to meet life's obstacles the way she met her own.

GO ON →

Answer these questions about "Bessie Coleman and Me."

15 Read the sentence from the passage "Bessie Coleman and Me."

Many people paid me compliments on my performance, including my brother Jeremy.

Which word from the sentence has a positive connotation?

Ⓐ paid

Ⓑ compliments

Ⓒ performance

Ⓓ brother

16 Write the missing words or phrases in the areas indicated.

The passage "Bessie Coleman and Me" is told from the point of view of the character named _____. It is written in _____ person.

17 What is the theme of the passage "Bessie Coleman and Me"? Use details from the passage to support your answer.

_____

_____

_____

_____

_____

GO ON →

Answer these questions about "Bessie Coleman."

18 Read the sentence from the passage "Bessie Coleman."

Bessie's popularity grew, and she became a local hero. She was even nicknamed "Queen Bess."

What is the meaning of the root in the word popularity?

(A) loved by many

(B) in charge of a lot

(C) given many names

(D) known in a small area

19 Why did the author **most likely** use subtitles in the passage "Bessie Coleman"? Pick **two** choices.

(A) to indicate the main ideas of each section

(B) to point out the most important details first

(C) to show the order in which events occurred

(D) to highlight the themes of the entire passage

(E) to focus on why learning to fly was so important

20 The passage "Bessie Coleman" says that no flight school in the United States would admit Bessie Coleman as a student. What are some of the ways this affected Bessie Coleman's life? Use details from the passage to support your answer.

_____

_____

_____

_____

_____

_____

GO ON →

Name: _____ Date: _____

Now answer this question about "Bessie Coleman and Me" and "Bessie Coleman."

21 Compare how the authors of the passages "Bessie Coleman and Me" and "Bessie Coleman" tell the Bessie Coleman story. In what ways are the passages different? In what ways are they alike? Use details from both passages to support your answer.

_____

_____

_____

_____

_____

_____

_____

_____

_____

_____

_____

_____

_____

_____

_____

_____

GO ON →

The passage below needs revision. Read the passage. Then answer the questions.

My Sister Nita and I

My sister Nita and I don't always agree, but we ___(1)___ alike in one way. We both really like dogs. Terriers and spaniels are my favorite dogs. Chihuahuas are ___(2)___ .

We ___(3)___ one big problem, though. Whenever we ask for a dog, our parents simply say, "No pets." They say that ___(4)___ jobs keep them too busy already. They don't want any more responsibilities.

We've tried to convince ___(5)___ that we are old enough to take care of a dog ourselves. We would feed it and walk it and pick up after it. One day we asked again.

"I know ___(6)___ would end up doing most of the work," said Papa. "And I just don't have the time."

"___(7)___ not being fair, Papa!" said Nita. ___(8)___ made her famous pouty face. But Papa didn't change ___(9)___ mind.

So Nita and ___(10)___ have made a plan. To prove that we're ready to take responsibility for a pet, we are starting a dog walking business. Posters advertising our dog-care services are going up tomorrow!

GO ON →

22 Which answer should go in blank (1)?

Ⓐ am

Ⓑ are

Ⓒ is

23 Which answer should go in blank (2)?

Ⓐ hers

Ⓑ his

Ⓒ ours

24 Which answer should go in blank (3)?

Ⓐ are

Ⓑ has

Ⓒ have

25 Which answer should go in blank (4)?

Ⓐ their

Ⓑ there

Ⓒ they're

26 Which answer should go in blank (5)?

Ⓐ their

Ⓑ them

Ⓒ they

GO ON →

27 Which answer should go in blank (6)?

Ⓐ whose

Ⓑ whom

Ⓒ who

28 Which answer should go in blank (7)?

Ⓐ You're

Ⓑ Yours

Ⓒ Your

29 Which answer should go in blank (8)?

Ⓐ He

Ⓑ She

Ⓒ They

30 Which answer should go in blank (9)?

Ⓐ his

Ⓑ her

Ⓒ its

31 Which answer should go in blank (10)?

Ⓐ myself

Ⓑ me

Ⓒ I

STOP

Narrative Performance Task

Task:

Your class has an upcoming field trip to a special museum, called a planetarium, which presents educational shows about stars and space. To prepare for this trip, you have been learning about stars, planets, constellations, and solar systems. Your teacher has asked everyone in the class to look up information about constellations. You have found two sources on the topic.

After you have reviewed these sources, you will answer some questions about them. Briefly scan the sources and the three questions that follow. Then, go back and read the sources carefully so you will have the information you will need to answer the questions and write a narrative paper.

In Part 2, you will write a narrative paper using information from the two sources.

Directions for Part 1

You will now look at the two sources. You can look at either of the sources as often as you like.

Research Questions:

After reviewing the research sources, use the rest of the time in Part 1 to answer three questions about them. Your answers to these questions will be scored. Also, your answers will help you think about the information you have read and viewed, which should help you write your narrative paper.

You may take notes when you think it would be helpful.

Your written notes will be available to you in Part 1 and Part 2 of the performance task.

GO ON →

Source #1: Stories Behind the Stars

The sky can seem endless. There are many things in the sky that we are not even able to see without powerful telescopes. Since there is so much that is unknown about the stars in the sky, they remain a mystery to many people. Native Americans are one group of people who thought the sky and stars were mysterious. Long ago, they created tales, called myths or legends, to explain the things they saw in the sky. They also used their myths and legends about the sky to teach lessons or provide entertainment.

Coyote Places the Stars

The Navajo tell a story about a time before the stars and the moon were in the sky. It was so dark that the animals would bump into one another. They asked the Great Spirit for help. The Great Spirit threw a shiny stone into the sky. The stone became the home star, which we now call the North Star. The Great Spirit then told the animals to take more shiny stones to the sky to make pictures of themselves. When they grew tired, the animals went to the coyote for help. The coyote thought he was the wisest and cleverest of all animals and did not want to help. But he didn't want to make the Great Spirit mad, so he lazily took stones and threw them into air. As the story teaches, that is why so many of the constellations do not appear finished. It is also why some do not look like what they are, and why so many are randomly scattered. The lazy coyote was in such a hurry that he didn't save any stones for his own picture. For this reason, the coyote howls at night.

The Spider and the Sun

The Cherokee also tell a story to explain what we see in the sky. This story also begins long ago, when there was no sun and it was always dark. The animals met about this problem. Woodpecker had heard that people on the other side of the world had light. Fox said that they must be too greedy to share it. Possum volunteered to go steal a piece of the light, planning to hide it in his bushy tail. When he did manage to hide a piece of Sun in his tail, it burned off all of his fur. That is why possums' tails are bald and possums only come out at night. Buzzard tried next, planning to balance the piece of Sun on his head feathers. But the Sun was so hot it burned off those feathers. The buzzard has remained bald since. Then Grandmother Spider offered to go. She spun a web on her way, placed a tiny bit of the Sun in the center of the web, and began

GO ON →

her way home. Since that time, the web of the spider is shaped like the disk and rays of the Sun, and both sides of the world share the light.

Walks All Over the Sky

The Tsimshian Tribe tell a tale of a chief with two sons. They were a younger son, One Who Walks All Over the Sky, and an older son, Walking About Early. The younger son was sad to see the sky always so dark, so he made a mask out of wood and tar and lit it on fire. This became the sun, and each day the younger son travels across the sky carrying it. At night he sleeps below the horizon, and when he snores, sparks fly from the mask and make the stars. The older brother became jealous. To impress their father, he smeared fat and charcoal on his face, becoming the moon, and now he makes his own way across the sky. Today, science and technology have provided other answers to questions about the sun, moon, and stars. But the stories that Native Americans and other ancestors told have many purposes. It is no mystery why the wonders of the universe inspired so many tales.

Source #2: Let the Stars Be Your Guide

"A real sailor only needs the stars." – The captain in White Squall

You jump in the car with your mom or dad, push a few buttons, and hear a voice calmly say, "Please start driving on the highlighted route." GPS is a modern way to find our way from one place to another. Long ago, people used stars as their GPS. This was called "celestial navigation."

For centuries, groups of people have been using the stars in the sky for many purposes. For example, Native Americans created myths and other stories to help explain what they saw in the stars in the sky. Sailors, too, have used stars for centuries to help them find their way. Even animals use stars to guide them.

How It Works

People and animals can figure out where they are on the earth by using the sun, moon, and stars. These objects are used because they are easy to locate. To use celestial navigation, people measure the height of these objects and learn how they move in the sky.

GO ON →

How Long Have People Used Stars?

For centuries, groups of people were able to find their way around the world using only the sky as their guide. These people used to use the sun and time of day to figure out where north, south, east, and west were. For example, in the morning, the sun can be found in the east. At night, people could find north by finding the North Star. The North Star is located directly above the North Pole, so it stays in the same spot in the sky while all the other stars appear to move in a circle around it. People could also figure out how far north they were by measuring the height of the North Star from the horizon.

Later, people realized that the stars move through the sky in certain ways and can be tracked. They used this information to create charts. These charts, along with special tools used to measure the height of stars, the sun, and the moon, made the job easier, but not perfect. For example, Christopher Columbus thought he had landed in a much different place than he really had because of his navigation.

Animals That Use Stars

People are not the only ones using what they see in the sky to find their way. A study found that one specific bird flies at night using the stars to guide it. Scientists also found that dung beetles use the stars in the Milky Way to find their way. They get lost when they can't see the sky.

The objects we see in the sky are beautiful tools we can use to help us find our way. There are times when we may be without modern tools to depend on. It is comforting to know that what we see in the sky could help us.

GO ON →

Name: _____ Date: _____

1 Both of these sources provide information about how stars have been useful for thousands of years. Draw a line from each source to choose **one** sentence in the list from Source #1 and **one** sentence in the list from Source #2 that best support this idea.

Source #1   "Today, science and technology have provided other answers to questions about the sun, moon, and stars."

Source #2   "This was called 'celestial navigation.'"

"For example, Christopher Columbus thought he had landed in a much different place than he really had because of his navigation."

"They also used their myths and legends about the sky to teach lessons or provide entertainment."

"Since that time, the web of the spider is shaped like the disk and rays of the Sun, and both sides of the world share the light."

"Sailors, too, have used stars for centuries to help them find their way."

2 Source #1 and Source #2 discuss how Native Americans created myths to explain what they saw in in the sky. What does Source #1 explain about how these myths were created that Source #2 does not? Explain why that information is helpful to the reader. Give **two** details or examples from Source #1 to support your explanation.

_____

_____

_____

_____

_____

GO ON →

3 Source #1 and Source #2 include information about how stars influence both people and animals. Explain what the sources say about how the stars have influenced both people and animals. Use **one** detail from Source #1 and **one** detail from Source #2 to support your explanation. For each detail, include the source title or number.

_____

_____

_____

_____

_____

GO ON →

Directions for Part 2

You will now review your notes and sources, and plan, draft, revise, and edit your writing. You may use your notes and go back to the sources as often as you need. Now read your assignment and the information about how your writing will be scored; then begin your work.

Your Assignment:

A few days before your class trip to the planetarium, a local author comes to your class and talks about the stories and myths she has written about stars and constellations. After her talk, she asks all students in your class to write their own myths or short stories about a constellation or star and says she will come back to the class and listen to all of the stories being read. Think about what you've read in the sources about constellations and stars and the stories and myths created about them. You choose to write a similar myth. What lesson will your myth teach? The story should be several paragraphs long.

Writers often do research to add realistic details to the setting, characters, and plot in their stories. When writing your story, use information and details about the stars from "Let the Stars Be Your Guide," and use characters or ideas from "Stories Behind the Stars" to help you develop your characters, setting, and plot. Use details, dialogue, and description where appropriate.

REMEMBER: A well-written story

• has a clear plot and clear sequence of events

• is well-organized and has a point of view

• uses details from more than one source to support your story

• uses clear language.

• follows rules of writing (spelling, punctuation, and grammar usage).

Now begin work on your story. Manage your time carefully so that you can plan, write, revise, and edit the final draft of your story. Write your response on a separate sheet of paper.

Question	Correct Answer	Content Focus	CCSS	Complexity
1A	B	Context Clues: Paragraph Clues	L.4.4a	DOK 2
1B	A	Context Clues: Paragraph Clues/ Text Evidence	L.4.4a/ RL.4.1	DOK 2
2A	C	Figurative Language: Idioms	L.4.5b	DOK 3
2B	A	Figurative Language: Idioms/ Text Evidence	L.4.5b/ RL.4.1	DOK 3
3	E, F	Context Clues: Synonyms	L.4.5c	DOK 2
4	B	Literary Elements: Stanzas	RL.4.5	DOK 2
5A	C	Point of View	RL.4.6	DOK 2
5B	A	Point of View/Text Evidence	RL.4.6/ RL.4.1	DOK 2
6A	A	Theme	RL.4.2	DOK 3
6B	A	Theme/Text Evidence	RL.4.2/ RL.4.1	DOK 3
7	see below	Literary Elements: Repetition	RL.4.5	DOK 3
8	A, B	Context Clues: Synonyms	L.4.5c	DOK 2
9	A	Latin Roots	L.4.4b	DOK 1
10A	C	Text Structure: Cause & Effect	RI.4.3	DOK 3
10B	C	Text Structure: Cause & Effect/ Text Evidence	RI.4.3/ RI.4.1	DOK 3
11	A, E	Text Features: Boldface Words	RI.4.7	DOK 2
12A	D	Context Clues: Paragraph Clues	L.4.4a	DOK 2
12B	A	Context Clues: Paragraph Clues/ Text Evidence	L.4.4a/ RI.4.1	DOK 2
13	see below	Text Structure: Cause & Effect	RI.4.3	DOK 3
14	see below	Text Structure: Cause & Effect	RI.4.3	DOK 3
15	B	Context Clues: Paragraph Clues	L.4.4a	DOK 2
16	see below	Point of View	RI.4.6	DOK 2
17	see below	Theme	RI.4.2	DOK 3
18	A	Latin Roots	L.4.4b	DOK 2
19	A, C	Text Structure: Cause & Effect	RI.4.3	DOK 2
20	see below	Text Structure: Cause & Effect	RI.4.3	DOK 3
21	see below	Compare Across Texts	W.4.9b	DOK 4

Question	Correct Answer	Content Focus	CCSS	Complexity
22	B	Pronoun-Verb Agreement	L.3.1f	DOK 1
23	A	Possessive Pronouns	L.3.2d	DOK 1
24	C	Pronoun-Verb Agreement	L.3.1f	DOK 1
25	A	Pronouns & Homophones	L.4.1g	DOK 1
26	B	Types of Pronouns	L.3.1a	DOK 1
27	C	Pronouns & Antecedents	L.4.1a	DOK 1
28	A	Pronouns & Homophones	L.3.1a	DOK 1
29	B	Pronouns & Antecedents	L.4.1a	DOK 1
30	A	Possessive Pronouns	L.3.2d	DOK 1
31	C	Types of Pronouns	L.3.1a	DOK 1

Comprehension: Selected Response 4, 5A, 5B, 6A, 6B, 10A, 10B, 11, 19	/12	%
Comprehension: Constructed Response 7, 13, 14, 16, 17, 20, 21	/16	%
Vocabulary 1A, 1B, 2A, 2B, 3, 8, 9, 12A, 12B, 15, 18	/16	%
English Language Conventions 22–31	/10	%
Total Unit Assessment Score	/54	%

7 **2-point response:** The author had the two characters running in the race use repeated phrases throughout the poem to stress the differences between the two characters. Tortoise's repeated lines show Tortoise's stick-to-it attitude about running the race, while Hare's repeated lines show how flashy and loud Hare was, and his obvious physical advantage over Tortoise.

13 Students should number the following events as shown:

1. Arthur Conan Doyle wrote stories that became very popular for a magazine.

2. Arthur Conan Doyle decided to write about what interested him most.

3. Arthur Conan Doyle was begged to continue writing the stories that made him famous.

14 **2-point response:** An American publisher offered Doyle $5,000 to write one story again about Holmes. Because it was so much money, Doyle agreed. No one knows for sure, but Doyle probably continued writing about Holmes because he realized how much money he could make and how much his characters were loved by the public.

16 Students should complete the sentences with the following words:
• Emily
• first

17 **2-point response:** The theme of the passage is how to have courage at times when you feel the worst. In this passage, the reader sees that learning about another person's courage can often help you feel brave too. Emily is really nervous and worried about how well she will do in the play, but when she reads about Bessie Coleman's hard work and determination, it helps boost her confidence, and she does a great job.

20 **2-point response:** The passage says that because no American flight school would accept Bessie Coleman as a student, Bessie Coleman moved to France to learn to fly. Later she wanted to open a flight school of her own that would be open to everyone, because she wanted to make things better for others in the future. She raised money for this by performing stunts in air shows, and she was killed during one of the stunts.

21 **4-point response:** While both passages focus on Bessie Coleman, in "Bessie Coleman and Me" she is a side character, but in "Bessie Coleman" she is the main character and focus. The passage "Bessie Coleman and Me" is mostly about a girl named Emily. Emily reads a book about Bessie Coleman. The passage briefly describes some of the obstacles Bessie Coleman had to face when becoming a pilot, but it uses those facts as inspiration for Emily to do a better job performing in the school play. Emily is very glad that she learned about Bessie Coleman, but the story goes into more detail about what is happening for Emily. On the other hand, the passage "Bessie Coleman" focuses on the entire life of Bessie, from birth to death. The obstacles Bessie had to face are just one portion of the passage. This passage provides a lot of information about Bessie Coleman and does a much better job of showing who she was, the struggles she faced, and her many accomplishments.

Narrative Performance Task

Question	Answer	CCSS	Complexity	Score
1	see below		DOK 3	/1
2	see below	RI.4.1, RI.4.2, RI.4.8, RI.4.9 W.4.3a-e, W.4.4, W.4.7 L.4.1, L.4.2	DOK 3	/2
3	see below		DOK 3	/2
Narrative Story	see below		DOK 4	/4 [P/O] /4 [D/E] /2 [C]
Total Score				**/15**

1 Students should draw lines to match the following statements:
- Source #1: "They also used their myths and legends about the sky to teach lessons or provide entertainment."
- Source #2: "Sailors, too, have used stars for centuries to help them find their way."

2 **2-point response:** While Source #2 mentions that Native Americans used the stars to create myths and teach lessons, Source #1 actually provides examples of those stories and how they explained the objects in the sky. By providing these different stories, Source #1 helps the reader better understand what lessons were taught and how they reflect the culture they came from.

3 **2-point response:** "Stories Behind the Stars" describes how Native Americans created myths and legends about the sky to help explain its mysteries. They also used these stories about the stars to teach important lessons. "Let the Stars Be Your Guide" includes information about how people and animals relied on the stars and other objects in the sky to navigate.

10-point anchor paper: Long ago, when the stars were first in the sky, none of them moved. They just sat where they were, some arranged into the beginnings of pictures, and some scattered randomly. During this time, Fox and Coyote went for a walk and got lost.

"Are we going the right way? I don't recognize the smells here," said Fox.

"I'm sure I'll recognize something soon," answered Coyote.

But the farther they went, the more certain they became that they were badly lost. Finally, they just sat down and howled at the top of their lungs for help.

Woodpecker heard them. "I will fly high above the trees to look for your home," she said. So she flew and flew. Finally, she found the valley where Fox and Coyote lived. She picked up a stone and placed it in the sky to mark the spot. In the process, she bumped the sky and set all the other stars spinning.

The stone that Woodpecker placed became the North Star, and to this day, it still marks the same spot, while all the other stars spin around it. Woodpecker used it to guide Fox and Coyote home, and other people and animals have used it to find their way ever since.

Read the passage. Then answer the questions.

The Santa Fe Trail

In the 1800s, many trails crossed the American West, and one of these was the Santa Fe Trail. Unlike most trails at the time, it was used mainly for trading. Other trails were used by settlers going to make a new life in the West.

For a while, Spain ruled the area around Santa Fe. The Spanish prohibited trade with the United States. However, after Mexico gained its freedom from Spain, trade between Mexico and the United States began. In 1821, William Becknell made a trip from Missouri to Santa Fe to trade. This was the first of many trips along the trail. The next year he came back with a wagon train full of goods. At its peak, the trail carried more than 2,000 wagons a year.

The trail was about 780 miles long, and it took 40 to 60 days to reach Santa Fe from Missouri. The trail followed the Arkansas River and then split into two paths. The first path went with the river to Bent's Fort in Colorado and then turned south through a mountain pass to reach Santa Fe.

The second path went southwest to New Mexico and crossed the desert to Santa Fe. This path was shorter and easier for wagon trains to follow. It did not go through mountains like the first route. The desert was riskier, however, because travelers could run out of water in the desert.

The Santa Fe Trail, 1850

GO ON →

The Pecos Pueblo

One of the last places the trail passed through was the Pecos Pueblo, which was a group of ruins. Some of the ruins were from an ancient settlement. Others were the remains of old Spanish missions. Stories about these ruins told of lost gold.

Like Santa Fe, the Pecos Pueblo was a trade center. The site was just right for trade because it linked the farming areas of the Rio Grande valley with the hunting areas of the plains. Around A.D. 800, many tribes came to trade, and they brought items such as buffalo hides, shells, pottery, and food.

Because of its value as a trading center, the Pecos Pueblo grew in size. About 2,000 people lived at the site between the years 1450 and 1600. They stayed in large buildings that were four or five stories high. They climbed ladders up to each floor, and these ladders could be pulled inside for safety.

The Arrival of the Spanish

In the early 1500s, Spanish explorers came upon the Pecos Pueblo. When the native people met the Spanish, they told them stories about a place called Quivera. This was a city to the east that was supposed to be made of gold. More than likely, they told this story so the Spanish would go look for it and leave them alone. Their idea worked, because the Spanish left to search for the lost city of gold. Of course, they never found it.

By the end of the 1500s, more Spanish had arrived. The Pecos Pueblo changed hands a number of times. While the Spanish were in control, they built a great church. This church did not survive for long, but another was built later. What is left of this church makes up the most impressive ruins at the site.

As the site kept changing hands, the people living there moved away because they were tired of the unrest. In 1838, the last people packed up and left. For most of the time the Santa Fe Trail was used, the Pecos Pueblo was a desert ruin.

The Santa Fe Trail was not used much after 1880. Once a railroad linked Santa Fe with other major trading cities, the trail was no longer needed.

Today, the trail attracts tourists instead of traders. Some people still study the trail to understand how it was used, and a small group of people even travel the trail each year as a way to honor its history.

GO ON →

1 The following question has two parts. First, answer part A. Then, answer part B.

Part A: Read the sentence from the passage.

The desert was <u>riskier</u>, however, because travelers could run out of water in the desert.

Which word is an antonym of <u>riskier</u>?

Ⓐ better

Ⓑ easier

Ⓒ safer

Ⓓ wider

Part B: Which sentence from the passage **best** supports your answer in part A?

Ⓐ "This was the first of many trips along the trail."

Ⓑ "The trail followed the Arkansas River and then split into two paths."

Ⓒ "It did not go through mountains like the first route."

Ⓓ "Some of the ruins were from an ancient settlement."

GO ON →

2 Read the sentences from the passage.

The Spanish <u>prohibited</u> trade with the United States. However, after Mexico gained its freedom from Spain, trade between Mexico and the United States began.

Which word has the **opposite** meaning of <u>prohibited</u> as it is used in the passage? Pick **all** that apply.

(A) allowed

(B) denied

(C) ignored

(D) outlawed

(E) permitted

(F) taxed

3 Read the sentence from the passage.

The first path went with the river to Bent's Fort in Colorado and then turned south through a mountain <u>pass</u> to reach Santa Fe.

Which meaning fits <u>pass</u> as it is used in the sentence from the passage?

(A) narrow route or road

(B) throw a ball, as in football

(C) permission to come and go

(D) move past or around something

GO ON →

4 The following question has two parts. First, answer part A. Then, answer part B.

Part A: Which of these events happened **first** in the history of the Pecos Pueblo?

(A) Spaniards began looking for Quivera.

(B) William Becknell traveled to Sante Fe.

(C) Pecos Pueblo became a trading center.

(D) Spanish missionaries came to Pecos Pueblo.

Part B: Which sentence from the passage best supports your answer in part A?

(A) "The next year he came back with a wagon train full of goods."

(B) "Around A.D. 800, many tribes came to trade, and they brought items such as buffalo hides, shells, pottery, and food."

(C) "Their idea worked, because the Spanish left to search for the lost city of gold."

(D) "While the Spanish were in control, they built a great church."

5 The passage says that the Santa Fe Trail followed the Arkansas River and then split into two paths. What were the problems with each path?

Draw lines to match **one** problem from the list with each path.

path through the
mountains

path through the desert

Less water was available
on this path.

Wagon trains had more
trouble following this path.

Hunting was more difficult
on this path.

Trade was prohibited on
this path.

GO ON →

6 The following question has two parts. First, answer part A. Then, answer part B.

Part A: The author describes how life changed at the Pecos Pueblo. What evidence from the passage shows the event that caused the **most** change?

(A) A church was built at the Pecos Pueblo.

(B) Spanish explorers arrived at Pecos Pueblo.

(C) Many tribes went to trade at the Pecos Pueblo.

(D) The Santa Fe trail passed through Pecos Pueblo.

Part B: Which sentence from the passage **best** supports your answer in part A?

(A) "One of the last places the trail passed through was the Pecos Pueblo, which was a group of ruins."

(B) "Around A.D. 800, many tribes came to trade, and they brought items such as buffalo hides, shells, pottery, and food."

(C) "As the site kept changing hands, the people living there moved away because they were tired of the unrest."

(D) "While the Spanish were in control, they built a great church."

7 What problems happened at the Pecos Pueblo, and how did the people living there try to solve those problems? Use details from the passage to support your answer.

_____

_____

_____

_____

_____

GO ON →

Read the passage. Then answer the questions.

First Day of School

It was the first day of school, and the hallways were buzzing and rattling with the sound of voices shouting back and forth, footsteps tromping, and lockers opening and closing. The sound and activity made it feel like a downtown train station at rush hour. Just to add to the confusion, an announcement came over the speakers that classes would be starting in five minutes. I was grateful I was not a new student this year and already knew where I needed to go for class.

Heading up the stairs, I noticed a girl standing to the side of the hall with Mr. Park, the vice principal. He looked worried, and the girl looked confused. I didn't recognize her—a new student, I thought. Trying to navigate the hallways and stairs was intimidating, especially if you're new.

"Is everything all right, Mr. Park?" I asked.

"Ah, Katherine, hello . . ." replied Mr. Park. He was clearly distracted and kept looking past me towards the school's front doors. "This is Maya Hanson, a new student," he added.

I smiled and said, "Hello there," but Maya did not respond. If anything, she looked more lost than she had a moment earlier.

"Oh, sorry Katherine," said Mr. Park. "Maya is hearing impaired and we are waiting for Cameron, her interpreter, to get here. He can then help her get settled into Mrs. Randall's class. Apparently, Cameron is running a bit late this morning. I'm afraid that while I can speak English and Spanish, I don't know a single word in sign language."

"Oh!" I exclaimed, suddenly understanding why Maya looked so lost. I tried to imagine what it would be like if I were standing in the hallway of a school where no one spoke my language. It would probably be uncomfortable. Then, I smiled, because I knew something that Mr. Park did not—I know sign language. Both my Aunt Helena and Uncle Joshua are deaf, so I learned how to sign when I was very small. Now I can hold entire conversations with my aunt and uncle, and I often interpret for them at family reunions or events.

GO ON →

Turning to Maya, I quickly signed, "Hello, my name is Katherine, and I can help you until your interpreter arrives."

Maya's face lit up with a huge smile, and she immediately responded, signing, "I am so glad to meet you—and that you know how to sign." Mr. Park looked quite pleased also, and he immediately asked me if I would be willing to walk with Maya to Mrs. Randall's room.

"We're in the same class," I told Maya, "so I can introduce you to everyone."

When we walked into Mrs. Randall's class, it seemed like every single student was talking, pulling out chairs, and dropping books. Since announcements were still being made, the noise level was incredible. I had an idea about how to lower the volume in the classroom and signed it to Maya, who grinned. She liked the idea as much as I did.

"Mrs. Randall," I said, walking over to our teacher, "I walked to class with Maya, one of the new students. We might have a way to get the class to quiet down."

Mrs. Randall smiled and welcomed Maya to the classroom, and then she stepped back. Maya and I went to the middle of the classroom and began signing to each other. It did not take long for students to notice and one by one, they stopped talking to watch us.

"That is so cool," said Steven.

"What are you two saying?" asked LaToya. "Can you show us how to do that too?"

"We can meet Maya and learn about sign language in a few minutes, but first I need to take attendance," said Mrs. Randall firmly. She started to close the door, but at the last minute, a young man slid through the opening and into the classroom.

"I'm Cameron Stewart, Maya's interpreter," he explained.

"Fine," said Mrs. Randall. "I will mark Katherine, Maya, and Cameron as present. Now, let's find out who else is here!"

GO ON →

8 Read the sentence from the passage.

The sound and activity made it feel like a downtown train station at rush hour.

What does this sentence suggest about the setting of the story? Pick **two** choices.

(A) There were people waiting in the hallways.

(B) There were stairs leading up from the hallways.

(C) The hallways were very noisy on the first day of school.

(D) There were many students moving through the hallways.

(E) There were announcements over the loudspeaker in the hallways.

9 Read the sentences from the passage.

"Ah, Katherine, hello . . ." replied Mr. Park. He was clearly distracted and kept looking past me towards the school's front doors.

Which words are antonyms of distracted? Pick **two** choices.

(A) alarmed

(B) confused

(C) focused

(D) interested

(E) worried

GO ON →

10 The following question has two parts. First, answer part A. Then, answer part B.

Part A: What causes Katherine stop to talk with Mr. Park as she walks through the hallway?

(A) She noticed that he did not look very happy.

(B) She wanted to ask how his summer had been.

(C) She wanted to ask him for directions to her classroom.

(D) She noticed that the announcements were not loud enough.

Part B: Which sentence from the passage **best** supports your answer in part A?

(A) "Just to add to the confusion, an announcement came over the speakers that classes would be starting in five minutes."

(B) "I was grateful I was not a new student this year and already knew where I needed to go for class."

(C) "He looked worried, and the girl looked confused."

(D) "Trying to navigate the hallways and stairs was intimidating, especially if you're new."

GO ON →

11 The following question has two parts. First, answer part A. Then, answer part B.

Part A: What conclusion can be drawn about the effect of Cameron's late arrival at school?

(A) It causes the students to be noisy in the hallways.

(B) It causes Maya to help Katherine open her locker.

(C) It causes the vice principal to walk students to class.

(D) It causes Maya and Katherine to start talking to each other.

Part B: Which sentence from the passage **best** supports your answer in part A?

(A) "It was the first day of school, and the hallways were buzzing and rattling with the sound of voices shouting back and forth, footsteps tromping, and lockers opening and closing."

(B) "I was grateful I was not a new student this year and already knew where I needed to go for class."

(C) "Turning to Maya, I quickly signed, 'Hello, my name is Katherine, and I can help you until your interpreter arrives.'"

(D) "When we walked into Mrs. Randall's class, it seemed like every single student was talking, pulling out chairs, and dropping books."

GO ON →

Name: _____ Date: _____

12 The noise level in Mrs. Randall's classroom was incredibly loud. What happened to lower the noise level? Pick **two** choices.

(A) Mr. Park came into the classroom.

(B) Maya and Katherine began signing to each other.

(C) Students stopped and watched the girls.

(D) Cameron arrived and closed the door.

(E) The morning announcements for the school began.

13 Read the sentence from the passage.

She started to close the door, but at the last minute, a young man slid through the opening and into the classroom.

Which definition from the dictionary entry **best** defines close as it is used in the sentence?

Dictionary Entry:
close (v) **1.** to shut **2.** to stop working **3.** to bring to an end
4. to reach an agreement about.

(A) to shut

(B) to stop working

(C) to bring to an end

(D) to reach an agreement about

14 What is a problem that the author addresses in "First Day of School"? Support your answer with details from the passage.

_____

_____

_____

_____

_____

GO ON →

Read the passages. Then answer the questions.

Lascaux: A Treasure in the Woods

One night in September 1940, four teenage boys headed for the woods near Montignac, a village in France. They set out, carrying a kerosene lamp and with a dog named Robot, to look for a cave. As they entered the woods, Robot ran ahead. The boys hiked along until suddenly, they heard Robot barking. The boys hurried toward Robot to find out what was wrong.

When the boys gathered around what looked like a rabbit hole to look for Robot, the earth collapsed under them. Shocked, they slid 50 feet down and landed in total darkness.

When 14-year-old Jacques Marsal lit the lamp and looked around, he was awed. There were animals painted all over the cave, and the paintings seemed to be moving.

The boys had stumbled into the caves of Lascaux. Inside these caves were some of the most remarkable cave paintings ever found.

Cave Art

These pictures were painted about 17,000 years ago during the Paleolithic Period, which is also called the Stone Age. Nobody knows why these images were painted, but we do know the people who created them were highly skilled.

The Lascaux painters used different colors to create depth and perspective. They also created some stunning effects by spraying paint onto the walls. Scientists suspect they blew paint through hollow bones or from their mouths. With this technique the colors fade together and create shadows. This is how the animals appear to move.

What the Boys Found

The Lascaux caves contain 850 feet of rooms and tunnels. The painted ceilings are 16 feet high in some places.

There are thousands of images showing humans, objects, and animals including horses, stags, bison, and wild oxen. They also show a rhino, a bear, and some big cats. This is amazing because some of these animals do not exist in France today.

GO ON →

The artists at Lascaux painted the animals they saw in real life. However, the Lascaux painters had to invent their own tools using bone and plants, the materials of their world. They made stone lamps and burned animal fat to create light so they could work in the dark caves.

To reach the ceilings, they created structures to stand on that were attached to the walls. To support these structures, they carved holes in the cave walls and attached poles. The structures were then built across the poles.

Hidden Treasure

Jacques Marsal, one of the boys who found the cave, never lost the feeling of awe. In fact, he devoted his life to protecting the paintings and became Chief Guardian of Lascaux.

When the boys found the caves, the paintings had been hidden for 17,000 years. The air and light in the caves had hardly changed in all those years. After the discovery, the world wanted to see these paintings. However, the people visiting the caves changed the temperature and light, which started to damage the paintings. To protect the paintings and the site, the caves were closed to the public in 1963.

Today, you can see photographs of the cave paintings and visit Lascaux II, which is a replica of two halls of the original cave. Only a few experts can visit the caves to see the paintings firsthand.

The paintings of Lascaux are a window to the past, and a picture is worth a thousand words. These paintings tell us a lot about how people lived during the Stone Age and how they saw the world around them.

GO ON →

Keys to the Past

Jill was discouraged when, after digging in the Buried City for two weeks, she had only observed the other students digging up artifacts. All she had discovered was a little metal disc with a man's head on one side, but everyone found those.

Suddenly, her trowel struck something hard, so she dug quickly, first with the trowel and then with her hands. The object had four sides, each about 15 inches long, and the back was about 7 inches high. In the front were several rows of flat, shiny buttons. Behind the rows was an array of thin metal rods arranged like a fan with tiny metal heads on the ends. Mounted in the back on top was a movable black cylinder with a wheel at both ends.

Jill dashed to Professor Quill's hut to show the artifact to him, but since he was gone, she left it with an assistant and walked slowly back to the site.

An hour later, Jill watched intently as Professor Quill and another man examined her artifact. "What do you think, Zap?"

"These people were hunter-gatherers," Dr. Zap said. "Perhaps they hurled it at animals."

"I don't think so," said the professor. "Look at the symbols on these buttons. They may have believed that touching these symbols would cause something magical to happen. Remember, this object is at least 4,000 years old, and the people who constructed it were extremely primitive."

"I doubt—" Dr. Zap began, but the professor interrupted him.

"Very good, Zap!" he said. "Doubt is the beginning, not the end, of wisdom."

Jill coughed politely, and everyone turned to look at her. "I found some more things," she said, holding up a box. The cover was slim and tattered, and hundreds of thin, white sheets were crammed inside. Jill removed a single sheet and asked politely, "May I try something?"

The professor nodded, so Jill walked to the artifact, pushed gently on a button, and one of the metal rods jumped up.

"I think these buttons are levers," she explained. "That little head on the end of the rod has the same symbol as the button I pressed."

GO ON →

Jill slipped the sheet behind the cylinder and turned the wheels so that the sheet wound around the cylinder and came up in front. She pressed one of the buttons, and a rod jumped up. It struck the sheet with a smack, causing a black mark, the same as the symbol on the button she had pressed, to appear on the sheet. She pushed down the next five buttons in the row, one by one, to create these marks:

qwerty

"Astonishing!" exclaimed Professor Quill.

"This gave me the idea." Jill removed a stack of sheets from the box. "These sheets are smaller and bound together along one side. They're nearly covered in the symbols. This seems to be a machine that produces symbols, perhaps for communication."

She handed the stack of sheets to the professor. The front and back were hard and shiny, and the front displayed a picture of a young boy and a one-legged man wearing a three-cornered hat.

Professor Quill lifted the front of the stack of sheets carefully. On the first sheet were only a few symbols that looked like this:

TREASURE ISLAND
by
Robert Louis Stevenson

"Remarkable!" said Professor Quill. "You have made an important discovery. We must attempt to figure out the meaning of these symbols."

GO ON →

Answer these questions about "Lascaux: A Treasure in the Woods."

15 Read the sentence from the passage.

These pictures were painted about 17,000 years ago during the Paleolithic Period, which is also called the Stone Age.

The root of Paleolithic is the Greek word "paleo," meaning old or ancient. What does this suggest that Paleolithic refers to?

(A) foreign people

(B) a time long ago

(C) the use of caves

(D) a time known for art

16 What information does the sidebar provide for the reader? Pick **two** choices.

(A) pictures of animals that no longer live there

(B) where Jacques Marsal is today

(C) where Lascaux is located

(D) how the painters made paint

(E) what is shown in the cave paintings

(F) tools used to create shadows

17 Explain the events that led the boys to find the cave paintings at Lascaux. Use information from the passage to support your answer.

_____

_____

_____

_____

_____

GO ON →

Answer these questions about "Keys to the Past."

18 Read the sentence from the passage.

"Doubt is the beginning, not the end, of wisdom."

What does this proverb **most likely** mean?

Ⓐ Having questions helps you learn.

Ⓑ The wisest people believe nothing.

Ⓒ The wisest people never have any worries.

Ⓓ You must start at the beginning to gain understanding.

19 The following question has two parts. First, answer part A. Then, answer part B.

Part A: What is the main problem that is mentioned in the passage?

Ⓐ The city is buried in dirt.

Ⓑ Nobody reads or writes any more.

Ⓒ The two archaeologists cannot agree.

Ⓓ The purpose of the artifact is uncertain.

Part B: Which sentence from the passage **best** supports your answer in part A?

Ⓐ "Jill was discouraged when, after digging in the Buried City for two weeks . . . ."

Ⓑ "I don't think so," said the professor.

Ⓒ "The front and back were hard and shiny, and the front displayed a picture of a young boy and a one-legged man . . . ."

Ⓓ "'We must attempt to figure out the meaning of these symbols.'"

GO ON →

20 In the passage, Professor Quill is not available to check Jill's artifact. How does this **most likely** change what happens after that moment in the passage? Use information from the passage to support your answer.

_____

_____

_____

_____

_____

_____

GO ON →

Now answer this question about "Lascaux: A Treasure in the Woods" and "Keys to the Past."

21 Compare the discoveries in the passage "Lascaux: A Treasure in the Woods" and the passage "Keys to the Past." Explain the similarities and differences using support from the passages.

_____

_____

_____

_____

_____

_____

_____

_____

_____

_____

_____

_____

_____

GO ON →

The passage below needs revision. Read the passage. Then answer the questions.

Small Town

My grandmother has ____(1)____ knowledge about this town than anyone. She's the ____(2)____ person I know. She has also lived here all her life. However, ____(3)____ facts can't explain how she knows so much. My ____(4)____ has lived here all his life, too. But his knowledge of history is ____(5)____ than mine.

GO ON →

22 Which answer should go in blank (1)?

Ⓐ morer

Ⓑ the more

Ⓒ moster

Ⓓ more

23 Which answer should go in blank (2)?

Ⓐ most thoughtfulest

Ⓑ thoughtfuler

Ⓒ most thoughtful

Ⓓ more thoughtfuler

24 Which answer should go in blank (3)?

Ⓐ the

Ⓑ those

Ⓒ a

Ⓓ this

25 Which answer should go in blank (4)?

Ⓐ good gray-haired, old granddad

Ⓑ old gray-haired, good granddad

Ⓒ old good gray-haired granddad

Ⓓ good old gray-haired granddad

26 Which answer should go in blank (5)?

Ⓐ badder

Ⓑ more bad

Ⓒ worse

Ⓓ worst

GO ON →

The passage below needs revision. Read the passage. Then answer the questions.

(1) "I just keep my eyes and ears open," Grandma says.

(2) "Don't we all do that?" I ask.

(3) "Most folks just see and hear," she explains, "but I try to look and listen."

(4) Surely that can't be her secret—or is it?

(5) "It is," she says. (6) "You want to know the true history of a small american town? (7) Talk to the people who live there. (8) They're smartest than you think. (9) The old folks can tell you things going back 60 or 70 years before you were born. (10) I'm good at letting folks talk. (11) I got to know our town. (12) This town is an very interesting place."

(13) I enjoy listening to my grandma talk. (14) I enjoy it more than anything else.

GO ON →

27 How can sentence 6 be written correctly?

(A) You want to know the true history of a Small american town?

(B) You want to know the true history of a small American Town?

(C) You want to know the true history of a Small American town?

(D) You want to know the true history of a small American town?

28 What is the best way to write sentence 8?

(A) They're smarter than you think.

(B) They're more smart than you think.

(C) They're most smarter than you think.

(D) They're more smarter than you think.

29 What is the **best** way to combine sentences 10 and 11?

(A) I'm good at letting folks talk, but I got to know our town.

(B) Because I'm good at letting folks talk, I got to know our town.

(C) I'm good at letting folks talk because I got to know our town.

(D) Letting folks talk, I'm good at getting to know our town.

30 What is the **best** way to write sentence 12?

(A) This town is a very interesting place.

(B) This town is the very interesting place.

(C) This town is this very interesting place.

(D) This town is that very interesting place.

31 What is the **best** way to combine sentences 13 and 14?

(A) More than anything else, I enjoy listening to my grandma talk.

(B) I enjoy listening more than anything else, and my grandma talks.

(C) My grandma enjoys listening and talking more than anything else.

(D) More than listening, I enjoy my grandma talking about anything else.

Informational Performance Task

Task:

Your history class has been learning about the many ways people learn about and remember the past. Your teacher has asked everyone in the class to look up information about the many ways to explore and learn about the past.

For this task, you will be writing an informational article about the ways people learn from the past. You have found three sources on the topic.

After you have reviewed these sources, you will answer some questions about them. Briefly scan the sources and the three questions that follow. Then, go back and read the sources carefully so you will have the information you need to answer the questions and write an informational paper.

In Part 2, you will write an informational paper related to the three sources.

Directions for Part 1

You will now look at the three sources. You can look at these sources as often as you like.

Research Questions:

After reviewing the research sources, use the rest of the time in Part 1 to answer three questions about them. Your answers to these questions will be scored. Also, your answers will help you think about the information you have read and viewed, which should help you write your informational paper.

You may take notes when you think it would be helpful.

Your written notes will be available to you in Part 1 and Part 2 of the performance task.

GO ON →

Source #1: A Moment in Time

Time capsules have often been used throughout history. They can be shoeboxes with childhood treasures buried in a backyard. They can also be air tight containers with vital records hidden inside buildings. No matter the scale, the main purpose of time capsules is to help future generations understand the past.

The information in time capsules can tell us what was happening at a point in history. But they can also tell us what people thought was important at that time. Recently, several time capsules have been discovered.

New York, New York

In 1914, New York businessmen buried a chest containing commercial directories and financial reports. These items were meant to celebrate the American Revolution and union of the colonies. Sadly, the chest was forgotten until the 1990s. It was then opened in May 2014. The New-York Historical Society, in turn, created its own time capsule. It contains materials meant to capture New York in 2014. These include hand sanitizer, ear buds, a subway card, and popular websites saved on a flash drive.

Boston, Massachusetts

A time capsule from 1901, found in Boston, Massachusetts, was opened in October 2014. The time capsule was sealed inside a lion statue that sits on top of the old statehouse building. Descendants of Samuel Rogers, who made the statue, had recently written a letter telling the City that the capsule was hidden there. The capsule included photos and autographs from government officials at the time. It also included newspaper clippings and political campaign buttons.

Baltimore, Maryland

A 100-year-old time capsule was discovered during the repair of Baltimore's Washington Monument. The capsule has not yet been opened. But research found that it contains programs from celebrations at the monument, local newspaper articles, and documents from the 100th anniversary of the Star-Spangled Banner.

GO ON →

Modern Value

Historian Dr. Yablon says that "disappointment is the most common response to time capsule openings." The contents of time capsules can be interesting, but they do not always lead to new knowledge. And now that technology allows us to save documents and photos so easily, it may not be necessary to save things in a sealed box. In fact, a modern version of a time capsule is being sent to Mars as part of a project by ExploreMars. The project has collected digital images and audio and video messages from millions of people on Earth. The project shows that the value is not just to those who receive the capsule. By choosing what to include, students learn how to decide what is important about their world. Kids learn about space by tracking the spacecraft and lander. They also learn that they are part of a global society.

Time capsules will likely always hold interest to those creating them and finding them. As described above, their value may be debated and may change over time.

Source #2: Digging into the Past

What comes to mind when you think of archaeology? Probably, dinosaurs and fossils buried in dirt, right? However, this field includes the study of many types of remains, or artifacts, to learn about life during another time. These can range from cooking tools to weapons to building remains from colonial villages to soil stains left by garbage dumps. Usually, archaeologists dig large holes in areas where societies have been present and remains might be found. Many of these excavation sites are explored for several years.

A wealth of information can be found by studying the remains left during both the ancient and recent past. A few of the main types of archeology are described below.

- **Prehistoric archaeology** provides information about cultures that did not have a written language or were not written about by others. This includes most of what happened more than 3,000 years ago. So, the only way to learn about these cultures is to unearth and study what they left behind.

GO ON →

- **Historical archaeology** is the study of cultures that existed during recorded history. This includes the study of art, religion, politics, social practices, and more.

- **Underwater archaeology** relates to remains that lie beneath oceans, rivers, and lakes. It includes the study of shipwrecks to understand how they were made and how water bodies affected the growth of cities and towns.

- **Industrial archaeology** focuses on the history of production. It includes artifacts such as bridges water power canals, and more. These materials show how industry changes over time. It is also a way to study how industry has affected things like travel, street design, and other aspects of life.

Each of these areas of archaeology teaches us about human history and culture. For example, fences at a site relate to how people divided property and shared resources. The location of stone spear points, sometimes found within animal fossils, can indicate where and when hunting took place. We can learn about the speed of changes in technology from industrial remains. Also, artifacts from the houses of the employees show how they were treated. Remains can tell us what types of food was eaten, how long people lived, how people spent their days, the size of families, and more.

Archaeology helps us understand where and when people lived on earth. It also shows why and how they lived. By studying artifacts, we can also learn how information was passed on from between civilizations and generations.

Source #3: Family History

More and more people every year are trying to track down their family history. The reasons they do this are varied. Whatever the reason, there are many resources people can use to dive into their pasts.

Keep It Relative
The first step to research your family history is a small one. Many people start by interviewing their own relatives. The oldest ones may have never relied on electronics to remember names and birthdates. So, they can often

GO ON →

remember information about many relatives. Old family books, such as Bibles and family record books, if there are any, can also be good sources. Many people used to record facts about family members in these special books. This could include names, birthdates, marriages, and more. And because family heirlooms were passed down, the information could cover many generations.

Close to Home

Another great resource is the local library. Directories and census counts held by the local library have information on names, birth dates, marriage dates, addresses and more. For families who have lived in one area for a long time, you may find family names in local newspapers. The library staff, which includes expert researchers, can also direct you to more resources.

Go Global

There are many groups that have taken information, with the help of local libraries and governments, and collected it in one big database. The information from these databases can be accessed online. People also can use websites to research family history. For a fee, these websites can do the legwork for you and research your family tree.

Why It Matters

There are many reasons why you may want to learn about your family history. Some people want to learn about and connect with their cultural heritage. In doing so, they discover the traditions of where they came from. You may find out that you are related to famous people, or you may find pictures of a great-uncle who has the same nose that you do! You may find that your relatives did something important, or discover that your family owns land in a far-off country. You may reconnect with long-lost relatives with whom you share a common history and bond. You also may find more about your family's medical history, which can help you take better care of yourself. Most people find that, by learning about their family, they are also learning about themselves. It often turns out that we all have more in common than we think.

GO ON →

1 Both Source #1 and Source #2 provide information on what items provide clues to how people lived on a daily basis. Draw a line from each source to choose **one** sentence in the list from Source #1 and **one** sentence in the list from Source #2 that best support this idea.

Source #1   These include hand sanitizer, ear buds, a subway card, and popular websites saved on a flash drive.

Source #2   In 1914, New York business men buried a chest containing commercial directories and financial reports.

Remains can tell us what types of food was eaten, how long people lived, how people spent their days, the sizes of families, and more.

By studying artifacts, we can also learn how information was passed on between civilizations and generations.

No matter the scale, the main purpose of time capsules is to help future generations understand the past.

It includes the study of shipwrecks to understand how they were made and how water bodies affected the growth of cities and towns.

2 Source #1 and Source #2 discuss how historical clues can help show how people lived in the past. Explain what the sources say about these clues. Use one detail from Source #1 and one detail from Source #2 to support your explanation. For each detail, include the source title or number.

_____

_____

_____

_____

_____

_____

GO ON →

3 Each source explains how to look into the past to learn about it. Explain why this information is important. Use one example from Source #2 and one example from Source #3 to support your explanation. For each example, include the source title and number.

_____

_____

_____

_____

_____

GO ON →

Directions for Part 2

You will now review your notes and sources, and plan, draft, revise, and edit your writing. You may use your notes and go back to the sources as often as you need.

Now read your assignment and the information about how your writing will be scored; then begin your work.

Your Assignment:

Your teacher is creating a bulletin board display to show what your class has learned about the importance of history. You decide to write an informational article about the many ways people can learn from the past. Your article will be read by other students, teachers, and parents.

Using more than one source, develop a main idea about the ways people learn from the past. Write an article that is several paragraphs long in which you explain the ways people can learn about the past. Make sure to have a main idea, to organize your article logically, and to support your main idea with details from the sources using your own words. Develop your ideas clearly.

REMEMBER: A well-written informational article:

- has a clear main idea
- is well-organized and stays on the topic
- has an introduction and conclusion
- uses transitions
- uses details from the sources to support the main idea
- develops ideas fully
- uses clear language
- follows the rules of writing (spelling, punctuation, and grammar)

Now begin work on your informational article. Manage your time carefully so that you can plan, write, revise, and edit the final draft of your article. Write your response on a separate sheet of paper.

Answer Key

Name: _____

Question	Correct Answer	Content Focus	CCSS	Complexity
1A	C	Context Clues: Antonyms	L.4.5c	DOK 2
1B	C	Context Clues: Antonyms/Text Evidence	L.4.5c/ RI.4.1	DOK 2
2	A, E	Context Clues: Antonyms	L.4.5c	DOK 2
3	A	Homographs	L.4.4c	DOK 2
4A	C	Text Structure: Sequence	RI.4.5	DOK 2
4B	B	Text Structure: Sequence/Text Evidence	RI.4.5/ RI.4.1	DOK 2
5	see below	Text Structure: Problem and Solution	RI.4.3	DOK 2
6A	B	Text Structure: Sequence	RI.4.5	DOK 2
6B	C	Text Structure: Sequence/Text Evidence	RI.4.5/ RI.4.1	DOK 2
7	see below	Text Structure: Problem and Solution	RI.4.3	DOK 3
8	C, D	Figurative Language: Similes and Metaphors	L.4.5a	DOK 3
9	C, D	Context Clues: Antonyms	L.4.5c	DOK 2
10A	A	Character, Setting, Plot: Cause and Effect	RL.4.3	DOK 2
10B	C	Character, Setting, Plot: Cause and Effect/ Text Evidence	RL.4.3/ RL.4.1	DOK 2
11A	D	Character, Setting, Plot: Cause and Effect	RL.4.3	DOK 2
11B	C	Character, Setting, Plot: Cause and Effect/ Text Evidence	RL.4.3/ RL.4.1	DOK 2
12	B, C	Character, Setting, Plot: Problem and Solution	RL.4.3	DOK 3
13	A	Homographs	L.4.4c	DOK 2
14	see below	Character, Setting, Plot: Problem and Solution	RL.4.3	DOK 3
15	B	Greek Roots	L.4.4b	DOK 2
16	A, E	Text Features: Sidebar	RI.4.7	DOK 2
17	see below	Text Structure: Sequence	RI.4.5	DOK 3
18	A	Proverbs and Adages	L.4.5b	DOK 2
19A	D	Character, Setting, Plot: Problem and Solution	RL.4.3	DOK 3
19B	D	Character, Setting, Plot: Problem and Solution/Text Evidence	RL.4.3/ RL.4.1	DOK 3
20	see below	Character, Setting, Plot: Cause and Effect	RL.4.3	DOK 3

Question	Correct Answer	Content Focus	CCSS	Complexity
21	see below	Compare Across Texts	W.4.9b	DOK 4
22	D	Adjectives That Compare	L.3.1g	DOK 1
23	C	Adjectives	L.3.1g	DOK 1
24	B	Articles	L.3.1a	DOK 1
25	D	Ordering Adjectives	L.4.1d	DOK 1
26	C	Adjectives That Compare	L.3.1g	DOK 1
27	D	Capitalize Proper Adjectives	L.4.2a	DOK 1
28	A	Adjectives That Compare	L.3.1g	DOK 1
29	B	Combining Sentences	L.4.1f	DOK 1
30	A	Articles	L.3.1a	DOK 1
31	A	Combining Sentences	L.4.1f	DOK 1

Comprehension: Selected Response 4A, 4B, 6A, 6B, 10A, 10B, 11A, 11B, 12, 13, 16, 19A, 19B	/16	%
Comprehension: Constructed Response 5, 7, 14, 17, 20, 21	/14	%
Vocabulary 1A, 1B, 2, 3, 8, 9, 15, 18	/14	%
English Language Conventions 22–31	/10	%
Total Unit Assessment Score	/54	%

5 Students should draw lines to match the following:
- path through the mountains: Wagon trains had more trouble following this path.
- path through the desert: Less water was available on this path.

7 **2-point response:** One problem that the people living at the Pecos Pueblo faced was that people might attack them. To prevent this, they stayed in buildings that were several stories high, with ladders up to each floor, and they pulled the ladders inside when they didn't want to let anyone in. Another problem was the arrival of the Spanish in the early 1500s. The native people tried to solve this problem by telling the Spanish about a city made of gold, to get the Spanish to go look for it and leave them alone.

14 **2-point response:** The author addresses the problem that sometimes plans go wrong and people need help. In the passage, Katherine's help solves a big problem for both Mr. Park and Maya and makes the first day of school much more pleasant for Maya.

17 **2-point response:** The boys were wandering in the woods when they accidentally fell 50 feet down into total darkness. When one of the boys, Jacques Marsal, lit the kerosene lamp, they discovered remarkable animal paintings all over the cave walls.

20 **2-point response:** If Professor Quill had been there when Jill found the box with shiny buttons, Jill might not have continued digging. But she did and found an item that seems to be a book. This allows her to figure out the purpose of the box.

21 **4-point response:** In the passage "Lascaux: A Treasure in the Woods," four teenage boys go out one night in 1940 into the woods near Montignac, a village in France. There they fall 50 feet down into a cave. The boys discover ancient cave paintings dating back 17,000 years. These paintings are of people and animals. The paintings reveal the everyday life of the people who lived there at that time.

The discoveries in the passage "Keys to the Past" take place in the future and reveal things about the people of the 20th century. These discoveries are not accidental. A group of students are digging in the Buried City, looking for artifacts of the past. One of the students, Jill, finds a box that dates back 4,000 years. She is uncertain what it is and leaves it for her professor. The two leaders, Professor Quill and Dr. Zap, argue over the purpose of the box. In the meantime, Jill continues digging, and she finds a stack of bound papers with symbols on them. She notices that the symbols on the box and the symbols on the sheets match. She is then able to figure out that the box is used to make the symbols on the sheets.

Informational Performance Task

Question	Answer	CCSS	Complexity	Score
1	see below		DOK 2	/1
2	see below	RI.4.1, RI.4.2, RI.4.9 W.4.2a-e, W.4.4, W.4.7 L.4.1, L.4.2	DOK 3	/2
3	see below		DOK 3	/2
Informational Article	see below		DOK 3	/4 [P/O] /4 [E/E] /2 [C]
Total Score				**/15**

1 Students should draw lines to match the following:
- Source #1: These include hand sanitizer, ear buds, a subway card, and popular websites saved on a flash drive.
- Source #2: Remains can tell us what types of food was eaten, how long people lived, how people spent their days, the sizes of families, and more.

2 **2-point response:** Source #1 mentions how time capsules included all kinds of clues, from financial reports to campaign buttons. The quote from Dr. Yablon points out that the contents of many time capsules are disappointing because the "do not always lead to new knowledge." Source #2 focuses on the types of clues archaeologists use to understand the past, but emphasize on clues are found in many places from in the ground to under the water.

3 **2-point response:** Looking into the past is important for a number of reasons. First, as it says in Source #2, it helps people understand the where, when, why and how people of the past lived. Secondly, it shows how information was passed from one generation to the next. In addition, as stated in Source #3, learning about the past, and one's descendants, helps people learn about and appreciate their cultural heritage.

10-point anchor paper: People can learn about the past in many ways. They can learn about their own family history or about the history of the country. They can use different sources to learn different things about the past.

One way people can learn about the past is by looking at things that people in the past meant for future people to find. Some people in the past created time capsules, which are containers of things collected to help future people understand the past. The passage "A Moment in Time" explains that the things in a time capsule could be financial reports, photographs, political campaign buttons, newspaper articles, or websites saved on a flash drive. Time capsules can be buried underground or in hidden places in buildings until they are found in the distant future. They can even be sent into space. But time capsules are often disappointing, because they do not necessarily reveal anything that people didn't already know about the past.

Name: _____

Another way people can learn about the past is by digging up artifacts like tools or garbage or the remains of buildings from long ago. This can tell us how people from the past ate, where and how long they lived, the size of their families, what technology they developed when, and how they treated one another. The passage "Digging into the Past" explains how archaeologists dig for artifacts left behind by cultures that did not have a written language and study the words written by cultures that did have a written language. Archaeologists even study artifacts from underwater, such as shipwrecks. They also study industrial materials from long ago to learn how industry changed over time.

A third way people can learn about the past is by researching their own family history. The passage "Family History" tells how people can interview their own relatives, look at old family record books, check libraries for old directories and newspapers, and look at online databases. They can even pay someone else to research their family history. By learning about their family history, people may learn about their medical history, discover famous relatives, or get in touch with relatives they did not know about before.

Learning about the past is important because it helps people learn about the present. No matter whether people are researching their own family histories, digging for artifacts, or opening time capsules, they are trying to find out more about how the past shaped the present.

Read the passage. Then answer the questions.

A Big New World

As the steam-powered train finally gasped to a halt, Hattie, eager to start her first visit to the city, grabbed her bag. She climbed down to the platform and quickly found her waiting relatives standing not too far from Uncle Harold's brand-new 1915 Model T Ford. As the group walked toward it, Hattie regarded Cousin Lillian's fancy clothes admiringly. However, she noticed that they did seem to make walking rather difficult.

Riding in the automobile was quite an experience as cars elbowed past like people at a crowded party. Because of the noise of so many horns blasting and the smell of the stinky fumes from all those engines, Hattie started to feel ill. When Hattie remarked on all this, Lillian was puzzled. "This is not a large amount of traffic," she said. "Are there many cars where you live?" She couldn't believe it when Hattie said that there were not many cars and that the small number of cars they had didn't all go out on the road at the same moment.

After a slow trip across town, they arrived at a tall brick house with a red front door. Inside, Aunt Mabel exclaimed, "Better late than never!" upon seeing them. Then she briskly steered Hattie into the warm front room, where Hattie was very happy to accept the welcoming arms of a big, soft armchair. She tried answering her aunt's questions but could not help yawning. Seeing that Hattie was completely exhausted, Aunt Mabel suggested an early bedtime and led her upstairs to show her around.

Hattie was amazed by the washroom upstairs. At home, the family took baths in a tub they carried into the kitchen and used water from the well that they heated on the woodstove. Because this was such a long process, they did not take baths often. Here at her relatives' home were both hot and cold water, coming right into the house, so you didn't have to preheat the water or carry anything!

During the night, Hattie woke to the sound of something clanking and hissing in her room. She cried out, frightened, and Aunt Mabel and Uncle Harold quickly appeared to learn what was wrong.

GO ON →

"That noise is only the steam in the radiator," her uncle said, pointing to a large metal object along the wall. "It's noisy. All these new houses heat with steam instead of fireplaces."

As her aunt and uncle walked back to their room, Hattie heard Lillian across the hall softly asking, "Hasn't she ever seen a radiator before?"

In the morning, Hattie stood in the kitchen doorway watching as the maid, Nora, cooked breakfast. The kitchen was very new and modern-looking, and the sink had hot and cold faucets just like the washroom. The white monster squatting in the corner turned out to be a refrigerator. The stove had metal coils that heated up when you turned some handles, and Nora said it ran on electricity, not wood. Hattie had heard about these inventions but had never seen them.

"Would you like some toast?" asked Nora. Mmmmmm! Hattie nodded. Nora attached the bread to a metal box with wire racks on the outside, plugged the metal box into the wall, and the wire racks started to glow.

"When one side gets brown, turn this knob to toast the other side," she said. "Watch carefully so it doesn't burn."

At home they made toast over the fire on a toasting fork, so Hattie knew about watching toast. How was this machine an improvement?

Hattie soon discovered that her relatives owned all of the latest gadgets. They also took pride in showing off their up-to-date city, and Lillian was amused when Hattie exclaimed about the modern marvels on every corner. To Lillian, all these devices were ordinary. She didn't understand that Hattie was seeing a new world—strange, exciting, and a little bit scary.

When Hattie returned to her home, she told her parents about all she had witnessed. "Some of those new gadgets and machines do make life easier. Sometimes, however, they're not any easier or they even cause problems."

Hattie's father replied, "The challenge is figuring out when a new way of doing something is really better. Now, how about some old-fashioned toast?"

GO ON →

Name: _____ Date: _____

1 Read the sentence from the passage.

As the steam-powered train finally <u>gasped to a halt</u>, Hattie, eager to start her first visit to the city, grabbed her bag.

What does the personification of the train as it "gasped to a halt" suggest that the train was doing? Pick **two** choices.

Ⓐ The train was making noises as it stopped.

Ⓑ The train was having a problem with its engine.

Ⓒ The steam that powered the train was being released.

Ⓓ The train was moving like a person who was exercising.

Ⓔ The train whistle was blowing to let people know it had arrived.

Ⓕ The train was making awful fumes that made the passengers sick.

2 Read the sentence from the passage.

Inside, Aunt Mabel exclaimed, "<u>Better late than never!</u>" upon seeing them.

What does the saying "better late than never" mean?

Ⓐ It is best to be patient when you are waiting for something to happen.

Ⓑ Everything in life seems to take longer than people expect or plan for.

Ⓒ Time seems to move very slowly when you are waiting for someone to arrive.

Ⓓ It is better for something good to happen after you expect it than not to happen at all.

GO ON →

3 Draw lines to match **two** sentences from the list that are examples of imagery from the passage.

Imagery

Imagery

"Riding in the automobile was quite an experience as cars elbowed past like people at a crowded party."

"Hattie soon discovered that her relatives owned all of the latest gadgets."

"Hattie was amazed by the washroom upstairs."

"However, she noticed that they did seem to make walking rather difficult."

"The white monster squatting in the corner turned out to be a refrigerator."

4 Which words from the passage are homophones? Draw lines to mark **two** pairs of homophones.

homophones

homophones

knew/new

made/maid

nodded/not

soon/sound

were/wire

GO ON →

5 The following question has two parts. First, answer part A. Then, answer part B.

Part A: Read the sentence from the passage.

Here at her relatives' home were both hot and cold water, coming right into the house, so you didn't have to preheat the water or carry anything!

What does the word preheat mean as it is used in the sentence?

(A) to heat water fully

(B) to heat water after

(C) to heat water again

(D) to heat water before

Part B: Which sentence from the passage **best** supports your answer in part A?

(A) ". . . carried into the kitchen . . ."

(B) ". . . water from the well . . ."

(C) ". . . on the woodstove."

(D) ". . . take baths often."

GO ON →

6 The following question has two parts. First, answer part A. Then, answer part B.

Part A: Which sentence **best** describes the lesson Hattie learns in the passage?

(A) Family members enjoy having visitors.

(B) Traveling by train is better than by car.

(C) New inventions sometimes make life easier.

(D) Life in a city is nearly the same as in a small town.

Part B: Which sentence from the passage **best** supports your answer in part A?

(A) "Because of the noise of so many horns blasting and the smell of the stinky fumes from all those engines, Hattie started to feel ill."

(B) "Seeing that Hattie was completely exhausted, Aunt Mabel suggested an early bedtime and led her upstairs to show her around."

(C) "Here at her relatives' home were both hot and cold water, coming right into the house, so you didn't have to preheat the water or carry anything!"

(D) "She cried out, frightened, and Aunt Mabel and Uncle Harold quickly appeared to learn what was wrong."

GO ON →

7 Read the paragraph from the passage.

After a slow trip across town, they arrived at a tall brick house with a red front door. Inside, Aunt Mabel exclaimed, "Better late than never!" upon seeing them. Then she briskly steered Hattie into the warm front room, where Hattie was very happy to accept the welcoming arms of a big, soft armchair. She tried answering her aunt's questions but could not help yawning. Seeing that Hattie was completely exhausted, Aunt Mabel suggested an early bedtime and led her upstairs to show her around.

How does the author's use of imagery and personification add to the passage? Use details from the paragraph to support your answer.

_____

_____

_____

_____

_____

GO ON →

Read the passage. Then answer the questions.

A Family Business

"Are you *still* using a fountain pen?" asked Lucas, walking into his sister's bedroom. He stood next to the desk and watched her write a letter to their grandmother in California. "Why in the world would you do that when you could use one of the dozen or so computers in Dad's workshop? No one even knows what a fountain pen is anymore."

As he scowled at Emily, he tried not to let her see that while he thought what she was doing was ridiculously old-fashioned, he also had to admit that her penmanship was remarkable. The letters flowed across the page beautifully so that it looked more like an art project than a letter. Still, it was so slow using a pen. There were no delete or back buttons for getting rid of mistakes. And, for goodness' sake—the Henderson family business was repairing computers. There were towers, monitors, and keyboards all over the house since Mr. Henderson tended to bring his work home with him.

"Grandma Patricia likes it when I handwrite her letters," Emily explained. "Plus, this pen has been in the family for three generations. It whispers of the past when I use it. Grandma was given it on her 13th birthday and then gave it to Mom when she turned 13. In turn, Mom gave it to me on my 13th birthday."

"You're absolutely right, Em," said Mrs. Henderson, sticking her head in Emily's doorway. "And Lucas, if you think about it, this family *is* all about communication." Emily glanced at Lucas out of the corner of her eye, but he looked as confused as she was.

"Come into the living room for a moment, and I will show you both what I mean," their mother said.

When Lucas and Emily walked into the living room and sat down on the couch, their mother brought out a photograph album that neither one of them recognized.

"This photo album contains pictures from your great-grandfather's business," explained Mrs. Henderson. "He sold some of the first telephones in Oregon."

"What is this guy doing?" said Lucas, pointing at a photograph of a man talking into a mouthpiece and holding a speaker to his ear.

GO ON →

Mrs. Henderson laughed. "He is talking on the phone, Luke, but that style of phone was called a candlestick phone. The ear piece and mouth piece were separate. When Great-Grandpa Henry starting selling these," she said, pointing to a rotary dial phone, "he thought they were astonishing."

She flipped through a few more pages of the album. "Great-Grandpa had that store for years, and then his daughter, your Grandma Patricia, started working for him. She was a hurricane when it came to sales." She turned the page to show a woman standing next to a table full of phones that seemed more familiar because they had buttons for numbers instead of dials.

"What are those boxes next to the phones?" asked Emily.

"Answering machines," replied Mrs. Henderson. "They had small tapes in them that recorded the messages people left."

"Today, your father is still in the communications business," continued their mother. "He repairs computers, which, as you know, are one of the main ways people stay in touch in this modern age. But even though most communication is now done in seconds with a few clicks of the mouse, we should still appreciate what came before," Mrs. Henderson added.

"Like my fountain pen," said Emily, and Mrs. Henderson nodded.

"That pen is a way of connecting one generation to the next. Perhaps you will give it to your child when he or she turns 13, Em."

Just then, the front door opened and Jeremy, Emily and Lucas's older brother, came into the living room. "I finally got a job," he announced loudly, as he tossed his backpack onto the end table.

"Congratulations, Jeremy! Where will you be working?" asked Mrs. Henderson.

"The cell phone kiosk at the mall," replied Jeremy.

Emily and Lucas burst out laughing, to the surprise of their older brother. "The family tradition continues," said Lucas.

"Here—look through this album and you will understand what we are talking about," said Emily as she handed the photograph album to her confused brother. "Now—I'm going back to my room to finish my letter to Grandma Patricia—and ask her about selling phones. Maybe I can get some tips for you, Jeremy," she added with a grin.

GO ON →

8 Read the sentence from the passage.

As he scowled at Emily, he tried not to let her see that while he thought what she was doing was ridiculously old-fashioned, he also had to admit that her penmanship was <u>remarkable</u>.

Which word has a connotation that is **most** similar to that of the word <u>remarkable</u>?

Ⓐ possible

Ⓑ incredible

Ⓒ noticeable

Ⓓ understandable

9 Read the sentence from the passage.

It <u>whispers of the past</u> when I use it.

When Emily uses the phrase "whispers of the past," what does that suggest about her? Pick **two** choices.

Ⓐ It demonstrates that Emily uses the pen very little.

Ⓑ It proves that Emily writes better when using the pen.

Ⓒ It emphasizes that Emily cares about the history of the pen.

Ⓓ It indicates that Emily sees the pen as a link to her ancestors.

Ⓔ It shows that Emily is embarrassed about using such an old pen.

10 Which words from the passage are homophones? Draw lines to mark **two** pairs of homophones.

homophones	ear/are
homophones	house/how's
	knows/nose
	left/let
	write/right

11 Read the sentence from the passage.

She was a hurricane when it came to sales.

What does this statement show about Grandma Patricia? Pick **two** choices.

(A) She caused the store to be untidy.

(B) She was unfriendly when in the store.

(C) She moved around the store very quickly.

(D) She changed the placement of all the phones.

(E) She was able to sell a lot of phones in the store.

(F) She increased business because she was full of energy.

GO ON →

12 The following question has two parts. First, answer part A. Then, answer part B.

Part A: Which sentence **best** states the author's message?

(A) Paying attention to the past while moving into the future is important.

(B) Fountain pens are excellent items to hand down to close relatives.

(C) Telephones have changed a great deal over the last few decades.

(D) Honoring family members from past generations is important.

Part B: Which sentence from the passage **best** supports your answer to part A?

(A) "'Grandma was given it on her 13th birthday and then gave it to Mom when she turned 13.'"

(B) "'This photo album contains pictures from your great-grandfather's business', explained Mrs. Henderson."

(C) "'He is talking on the phone, Luke, but that style of phone was called a candlestick phone.'"

(D) "'But even though most communication is now done in seconds with a few clicks of the mouse, we should still appreciate what came before,' Mrs. Henderson added."

GO ON →

13 Which sentences from the passage **best** show the theme of the passage? Pick **two** choices.

(A) "There were towers, monitors, and keyboards all over the house since Mr. Henderson tended to bring his work home with him."

(B) "'And Lucas, if you think about it, this family *is* all about communication.'"

(C) "'They had small tapes in them that recorded the messages people left.'"

(D) "'That pen is a way of connecting one generation to the next.'"

(E) "Emily and Lucas burst out laughing, to the surprise of their older brother."

(F) "'Maybe I can get some tips for you, Jeremy,' she added with a grin."

14 In the passage, how does Mrs. Henderson use the photograph album to teach Emily and Lucas an important lesson? Use details from the passage to support your answer.

_____

_____

_____

_____

_____

GO ON →

Read the passages. Then answer the questions.

A History of the Bicycle

The bicycles we ride today are light, safe, fast, and fun. However, this has not always been so. The first bicycles were built in Europe and the United States in the early 1800s, and they were heavy, slow, and dangerous. These early bicycles were called Hobbyhorses and had heavy wooden frames and two wooden wheels. Riders had to push them forward with their feet. Using one was more like running than riding. In fact, the German word for these early bicycles means "running machines."

Soon, some people improved the Hobbyhorse. In Scotland, in about 1839, Kirkpatrick MacMillan added foot pedals that were connected to the rear wheel by long rods, which made it easier to move. About 30 years later a Frenchman named Pierre Michaux, along with his son Ernst, improved these foot pedals and added a crank to the front wheel. Their bicycle made cycling popular. Some historians question if Pierre and Ernst worked alone, but they are generally recognized as creating what we think of as the modern bicycle. However, it still needed more work.

The Michaux bicycle had a front wheel that was much larger than the rear wheel. It was faster than the Hobbyhorse, but it often toppled over. Unfortunately, the Michaux bicycle was as uncomfortable as the Hobbyhorse, and it also ground loudly along the roads. The heavy, wooden wheels rimmed with iron resulted in a very rough ride, which caused people to refer to the Michaux bicycle as the Boneshaker.

GO ON →

In the early 1870s, a high-wheeled bicycle called the Penny Farthing was developed in England. Like the Michaux bicycle, it had one very large front wheel and two small back wheels. On some bicycles, the front wheel was five feet high. These high-wheeled bicycles could go quite fast, but they were hard to handle and often threw their riders!

Later inventors further improved the bicycle. In the 1880s, bicycle makers stopped making the front wheels so large, and the bicycle as we know it soon came into being. Still, designers kept working to make bicycles safer, faster, and easier to use.

It is fortunate for us that people continued to improve the bicycle. Today's safe, comfortable bicycles are enjoyed all over the world and are widely used for transportation and exercise. Many people have contributed to making the bicycle what it is today. All the inventors of the bicycle should take a bow.

The First Bike?

Leonardo da Vinci (1452–1519) was a famous painter and an inventive genius. Leonardo studied how things worked in nature and filled notebooks with detailed drawings. He then used these studies to dream up new machines. His designs included a helicopter, a robot, and many other ideas. But did he also invent the first bicycle?

Experts were surprised when a bicycle sketch drawn by Leonardo was published in a 1974 book. The editor stated that the drawing was found in one of Leonardo's notebooks on the back of another drawing. However, the discovery caused a lot of argument. Many experts did not think the sketch looked like Leonardo's work, and some suggested it was produced by one of his students. Then a scholar who had examined the same notebook in 1961 spoke up. He said the drawing had not been there when he studied the notebook.

Today, most experts believe the bicycle drawing is a fake. We still are not sure who made it or when it was made.

GO ON →

How to Become a Professional Bicycle Rider

Ride On!

It is easy, when watching cyclists battle for position in the Tour de France on television every summer, to dream of being a professional bicyclist. You love riding your bike. You crest over hills. You lean around curves. You race through parking lots. Becoming a pro cyclist sounds great. But what does it take to become a pro?

Time and Dedication

As with any other sport, becoming a great cyclist takes enormous dedication and time. Many coaches believe it takes seven years of training before a cyclist is ready to enter a professional race. Seven years may sound like an incredibly long time, but it often takes that long to learn, train, and practice.

Many experts recommend that beginning cyclists who want to compete ride their bikes six days a week for at least two hours each day. If the weather is too cold or wet, you can use a stationary bike instead.

Fortunately, today's racing bikes are designed to be light and fast, rather than slow and heavy like history's first bicycles. Bicycles have changed greatly over the years, which has made it possible for cyclists to move much faster. However, you will still need strong muscles to ride in races. Biking is hardest on your leg muscles. However, you will need to have powerful arms and torso muscles as well. Lifting weights and doing regular exercises can help with this.

Participating in all kinds of sports is helpful as well. Just because you are dreaming of becoming a pro cyclist, do not stop doing things such as joining the track team, playing basketball with friends, and swimming laps in the school pool. Those sports will increase your muscle strength and fitness. In turn, this will make you a better cyclist.

All of the hours you dedicate to riding and exercising are not going to help you enough without also eating healthy foods. Many pro cyclists recommend eating fruits, vegetables, and lean meats or proteins. These foods will give your body the nutrition it needs to compete.

GO ON →

Biking with Friends

Biking is more fun with friends. Ask your buddies to ride with you and look into joining a local bicycling club. Listings for these groups are often found at community parks, cycling stores, or at school. If you get the chance to ride with cyclists who are faster and more experienced than you—do so. You can learn from them. They will help you challenge yourself to do a little better and ride a little faster. Being part of a club can also help you be more aware of local biking events. Taking part in these smaller rides can teach you a great deal about how you cope with time pressure and with competing with others.

After you have been riding, exercising, and participating in biking events you may wonder "What is next?" Give some thought to finding a coach. While you can search online for a local expert, consider asking at your favorite bike shop, checking with the members of the bike club, or asking your gym teacher at school. They might have excellent suggestions for finding a coach. Coaches can share knowledge, recognize where you need to improve, and inspire you to become better at cycling. Ride on!

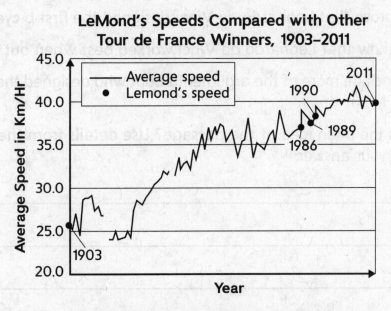

LeMond's Speeds Compared with Other Tour de France Winners, 1903–2011

(Note: 30 kilometers per hour equals about 19 miles per hour; the breaks in data show the years the race did not take place due to World Wars I and II.)

GO ON →

Answer these questions about "A History of the Bicycle."

15 Read the sentence from the passage.

However, the discovery caused a lot of <u>argument</u>.

What does the use of the word <u>argument</u> instead of the word "discussion" suggest about the experts?

(A) They agreed with each other.

(B) They had very strong opinions.

(C) They did not believe the editor.

(D) They were unsure about the truth.

16 Why was the sidebar included with the passage "A History of the Bicycle"?

(A) to describe some Leonardo da Vinci inventions

(B) to explain how the earliest bicycle came into being

(C) to add new information about the history of bicycles

(D) to prove that Leonardo da Vinci designed the first bicycle

(E) to show that Leonardo da Vinci worked best when out in nature

(F) to include more of the argument about who designed the first bicycle

17 What is the main idea of the passage? Use details from the passage to support your answer.

_____

_____

_____

_____

_____

_____

GO ON →

Name: _____ Date: _____

Answer these questions about "How to Become a Professional Bicycle Rider."

18 Read the paragraph from the passage.

Just because you are dreaming of becoming a pro cyclist, do not stop doing things such as joining the <u>track</u> team, playing basketball with friends, and swimming laps in the school pool.

The word <u>track</u> has multiple meanings. What does the word <u>track</u> **most likely** mean as it is used in the passage "How to Become a Professional Bicycle Rider"?

Ⓐ for running

Ⓑ a path to follow

Ⓒ a set of classes someone is offered

Ⓓ a mark to show where something was

19 Since the beginning of bicycle racing, the structure of the bicycle has been improved for racing.

What evidence from the graph **best** supports this inference? Draw lines to match **two** statements from the list.

bicycle structure	Bicycle riders must become faster and faster each year in order to win.
bicycle structure	The tires on bicycles are completely changed.
	A bicycle is presented that has less weight.
	Training materials for bicycle riders are published.
	Race developers introduce speed setting races.
	Some races take days to complete.
	A bicycle is introduced with tires made of a different material than the frame.

GO ON →

20 In the passage "How to Become a Professional Bicycle Rider," what is some of the most important information the author provides about training to be a professional cyclist? Use details from the passage to support your answer.

_____

_____

_____

_____

_____

GO ON →

Name: _____ Date: _____

Now answer this question about "A History of the Bicycle" and "How to Become a Professional Bicycle Rider."

21 What do the passages "A History of the Bicycle" and "How to Become a Professional Bicycle Rider" show about the amount of dedication and thought that went into the design of the bicycle? Support your answer with details from **both** passages.

_____

_____

_____

_____

_____

_____

_____

_____

_____

_____

_____

_____

_____

GO ON →

The passage below needs revision. Read the passage. Then answer the questions.

Grandmother from Java

(1) Grandma moved to the United States many years ago. (2) She learned right away that foods were different here. (3) She couldn't hardly find some of the ingredients she needed for her recipes. (4) She had to do her best with whatever she could buy in the market. (5) For example, one of her favorite dishes is a spicy soup called *tongseng*. (6) On Java the island where she grew up, this is usually made, with goat meat. (7) You can't buy goat meat in most American stores. (8) Grandma started making *tongseng* with lamb or beef instead. (9) Her *tongseng* tastes the more yummy of all the soups in the world. (10) I'm happy that it is part of my family background.

GO ON →

22 What information does the prepositional phrase in sentence 1 provide?

Ⓐ where Grandma moved

Ⓑ why Grandma moved

Ⓒ when Grandma moved

Ⓓ how Grandma moved

23 How can sentence 3 be written correctly?

Ⓐ She could not hardly find some of the ingredients she needed for her recipes.

Ⓑ She couldn't not find some of the ingredients she needed for her recipes.

Ⓒ She couldn't find some of the ingredients she needed for her recipes.

Ⓓ She couldn't find none of the ingredients she needed for her recipes.

24 Which is a prepositional phrase in sentence 4?

Ⓐ had to

Ⓑ do her best

Ⓒ whatever she could buy

Ⓓ in the market

GO ON →

25 How can sentence 6 be written correctly?

  (A) On Java the island where she grew up this is usually made with goat meat.

  (B) On Java, the island where she grew up this is usually made with goat meat.

  (C) On Java the island, where she grew up this is usually made with goat meat.

  (D) On Java, the island where she grew up, this is usually made with goat meat.

26 How can sentence 9 be written correctly?

  (A) Her *tongseng* tastes the yummier of all the soups in the world.

  (B) Her *tongseng* tastes the yummiest of all the soups in the world.

  (C) Her *tongseng* tastes the more yummier of all the soups in the world.

  (D) Her *tongseng* tastes the most yummiest of all the soups in the world.

GO ON →

The passage below needs revision. Read the passage. Then answer the questions.

One day in 1941, Georges de Mestral was out hiking in the Swiss woods. Stopping to rest, he found a lot of burrs sticking firmly __(1)__ his clothes. His dog's shaggy coat was covered with the pesky seed pods, too, and they __(2)__ come off easily. De Mestral studied the burrs __(3)__. Their surfaces were covered with a lot of tiny hooks. This gave de Mestral an idea. The burrs could provide a new way to fasten clothing. People needed something that worked __(4)__ than zippers. Zippers often broke or got stuck.

De Mestral started trying out different ideas. He finally came up with a strip of tiny nylon loops that would grab __(5)__ onto a strip of tiny nylon hooks. In 1955, de Mestral registered his invention under the name Velcro.

GO ON →

27 Which answer should go in blank (1)?

(A) beside

(B) for

(C) to

28 Which answer should go in blank (2)?

(A) didn't not

(B) didn't hardly

(C) did not

29 Which answer should go in blank (3)?

(A) careful

(B) carefully

(C) more careful

30 Which answer should go in blank (4)?

(A) better

(B) more better

(C) more good

31 Which answer should go in blank (5)?

(A) most tighter

(B) tightly

(C) tightest

Opinion Performance Task

Task:
Your class has an upcoming field trip to a local wind farm. To prepare for this trip, you have been learning about how wind power can generate electricity. Your teacher has asked everyone in the class to look up information on the differences between renewable and non-renewable energy sources. You have found two sources on the topic.

After you have reviewed these sources, you will answer some questions about them. Briefly scan the sources and the three questions that follow. Then, go back and read the sources carefully so you will have the information you will need to answer the questions and write an opinion paper.

In Part 2, you will write an opinion paper using information from the two sources.

Directions for Part 1
You will now look at the two sources. You can look at either of the sources as often as you like.

Research Questions:
After reviewing the research sources, use the rest of the time in Part 1 to answer three questions about them. Your answers to these questions will be scored. Also, your answers will help you think about the information you have read and viewed, which should help you write your opinion paper.

You may take notes when you think it would be helpful.

Your written notes will be available to you in Part 1 and Part 2 of the performance task.

GO ON →

Source #1: Energy Efficiency and Conservation

Energy is another word for power. Energy efficiency means using energy wisely. By saving energy, we are saving money. We are buying less fuel, saving resources, and creating less pollution.

Efficiency

Each job that needs power uses a different amount of energy. These jobs range from lighting a room to operating a video game system to powering a piece of equipment at a factory. As you can imagine, there are millions of different pieces of equipment and machines that use electricity and other types of energy.

Many types of fuels used to produce electricity have become more costly and hard to find. For this reason, people are trying to make machines that use less energy. For example, new types of light bulbs use less energy than older types of light bulbs to produce the same amount of light. Energy efficiency is so important that the United States Department of Energy now has an Office of Energy Efficiency and Renewable Energy. This office teaches people about using energy wisely.

The United States Environmental Protection Agency (USEPA) also has a program called Energy Star. Through the program, appliances that are more efficient than others are labeled with an Energy Star sticker. People buying appliances can use the sticker to help them find more efficient appliances.

Conservation

Energy conservation means using less energy. It is closely related to energy efficiency. There are things everyone can do to conserve energy. A few examples are:

• Turn off lights when you leave a room.

• Use sunlight instead of electric lights whenever you can.

• If the heat or air conditioning is on, close windows and doors to keep that air inside the building.

• Decide what you want to eat before opening the refrigerator door so that the cool air has less time to escape.

Many government agencies and companies have tools to help people calculate how much energy they are using. People can then change their habits or appliances to save electricity and power.

Always Improving

The largest use of electricity in homes is for air conditioning. Next is lighting and large appliances, like ovens. Lighting is the largest use of electricity in schools, stores, and other public buildings. It is easy to see that increased energy efficiency can help save a lot of electricity. Companies now look for ways to make appliances and other machines more efficient. Because saving energy means saving money and creating less pollution, people have many reasons to be efficient and use power wisely.

GO ON →

Source #2: Renewable Energy Sources: How They Are Used in the United States

The following information is part of a presentation on how renewable energy sources are used in the United States.

Renewable Energy Sources
How They Are Used in the United States

Renewable Energy

- Renewable energy sources are those that are not consumed or used up.

- Renewable energy sources can be used to provide heat and make electricity.

GO ON →

Renewable Energy

- The five main types of renewable energy are:
- Biomass
- Hydropower
- Geothermal
- Wind
- Solar

<u>Biomass</u>

- Biomass is material from plants and animals.
- Examples: wood, wood waste, crops, trash, animal manure, human sewage, and biofuels (ethanol, biodiesel).

- When biomass is burned, energy is released as heat.
- Gas that is released from biomass can also be used as energy.
- In 2013, biomass provided about **1.5%** of the energy used in the United States to make electricity.

GO ON →

Hydropower

- Hydropower is capturing energy from moving water.

- The first hydroelectric power plant in the United States opened in 1882.

- Hydropower is the largest renewable resource for making electricity in the United States.

- In 2013, hydropower provided about **7%** of the energy used in the United States for electricity generation.

Geothermal

- The word geothermal comes from the Greek words *geo,* meaning earth, and *therme,* meaning heat.
- Geothermal energy comes from heat—like steam or hot water—from the earth.
- There are more geothermal power plants in the western United States and Hawaii where geothermal energy sources are closer to the earth's surface.
- In 2013, geothermal sources provided about **0.4%** of the energy used in the United States for making electricity.

GO ON →

Wind

- Wind turbines, which are like windmills, use blades to collect energy from the wind.
- In recent years, wind is the fastest growing source of electricity in the United States.
- By 2011, 36 different states had large wind turbines.
- In 2013, wind sources provided about **4%** of the energy used in the United States for electricity generation.

Solar

- Solar energy is energy from the sun.
- Solar energy can provide electricity to individual houses or create electricity at a power plant for large areas.
- Solar energy could be a huge source of power. If just 4% of the world's desert areas were covered with panels to collect solar energy, the entire world could be supplied with energy.
- In 2013, solar energy provided about **0.2%** of the energy used in the United States for making electricity.

GO ON →

Use of Renewable Energy in the United States

- Wood has been used as a fuel for thousands of years.

- Fossil fuels—like coal, petroleum, natural gas—replaced wood as a primary energy source over time.

- As fossil fuels become harder and more expensive to find, renewable energy sources have become more popular.

- Today, more than half of renewable energy is used for producing electricity.

- In 2012, **12%** of electricity was generated from renewable energy sources. This is equal to about 45 million households. More than half of this was from hydropower.

Some Benefits of Renewable Energy

- Generally, renewable energy sources produce less air pollution than non-renewable energy sources (fossil fuels). This includes the pollution that causes climate change.

- While fossil fuels become more expensive and difficult to find, renewable energy sources will never run out.

- By burning trash, less waste is placed into overcrowded landfills.

Some Drawbacks to Renewable Energy

- Dams used for hydropower may obstruct fish migration and change these habitats.

- Some people feel that wind turbines ruin the view and are too noisy.

- A large area of land is required to capture enough solar energy to provide large amounts of electricity.

- While renewable energy sources do not run out, their supply is not constant.

GO ON →

1 Both sources provide information about the main problem with using traditional fuel sources. Draw a line from each source to choose **one** sentence in the list from Source #1 and **one** sentence in the list from Source #2 that **best** support this idea.

Source #1   Wood has been used as a fuel for thousands of years.

Source #2   Companies now look for ways to make appliances and other machines more efficient.

As fossil fuels become harder and more expensive to find, renewable energy sources have become more popular.

Many types of fuel used to produce electricity have become more costly and hard to find.

Fossil fuels—like coal, petroleum, natural gas—replaced wood as a primary energy source over time.

2 Both Source #1 and Source #2 discuss energy sources. What does Source #2 explain about energy sources that Source #1 does not? Explain why that information is helpful for the reader. Give **two** details or examples from Source #2 to support your explanation.

_____

_____

_____

_____

_____

GO ON →

3 Each source explains the concept of energy resources. Explain why knowing where energy comes from and how it is used is important. Use **one** example from Source #1 and **one** example from Source #2 to support your explanation. For each example, include the source title and number.

_____

_____

_____

_____

GO ON →

Directions for Part 2

You will now review your notes and sources, and plan, draft, revise, and edit your writing. You may use your notes and go back to the sources as often as you need.

Now read your assignment and the information about how your writing will be scored; then begin your work.

Your Assignment:

A few days before your class trip to the wind farm, your teacher asks all students in your class to write their opinion about how the school should reduce its energy usage. These opinion papers will be read by your classmates, your teacher, and the principal.

Your assignment is to use information from the sources to write an opinion paper about the best ways the school can reduce the amount of energy it uses. Make sure you clearly state your opinion with reasons and details from the sources. Develop your ideas clearly and use your own words, except when quoting directly from the sources. Be sure to give the source title or number for the details or facts you use.

REMEMBER: A well-written opinion paper:

- has a clear opinion
- is well-organized and stays on the topic
- has an introduction and conclusion
- uses transitions
- uses details or facts from more than one source to support your opinion
- gives details or facts from the sources in your own words
- gives the title of number of the source for the details or facts you included
- develops ideas clearly
- uses clear language
- follows rules of writing (spelling, punctuation, and grammar usage)

Now begin work on your opinion paper. Manage your time carefully so that you can plan, write, revise, and edit the final draft of your opinion paper. Write your response on a separate sheet of paper.

STOP

Name: _____

Question	Correct Answer	Content Focus	CCSS	Complexity
1	A, C	Literary Elements: Personification	RL.4.5	DOK 2
2	D	Proverbs and Adages	L.4.5b	DOK 2
3	see below	Literary Elements: Imagery	RL.4.5	DOK 3
4	see below	Homophones	L.4.4a	DOK 2
5A	D	Latin and Greek Prefixes	L.4.4b	DOK 2
5B	C	Latin and Greek Prefixes/Text Evidence	L.4.4b/ RL.4.1	DOK 2
6A	C	Theme	RL.4.2	DOK 2
6B	C	Theme/Text Evidence	RL.4.2/ RL4.1	DOK 2
7	see below	Literary Elements: Imagery	RL.4.5	DOK 3
8	B	Connotation and Denotation	L.4.5	DOK 2
9	C, D	Literary Elements: Imagery	RL.4.5	DOK 2
10	see below	Homophones	L.4.4a	DOK 2
11	E, F	Figurative Language: Metaphors	L.4.5a	DOK 3
12A	A	Theme	RL.4.2	DOK 2
12B	D	Theme/Text Evidence	RL.4.2/ RL4.1	DOK 2
13	B, D	Theme	RL.4.2	DOK 2
14	see below	Theme	RL.4.2	DOK 3
15	B	Connotation and Denotation	L.4.5	DOK 2
16	C, F	Text Features: Sidebars	RI.4.7	DOK 2
17	see below	Main Idea and Key Details	RI.4.2	DOK 3
18	B	Homophones	L.4.4a	DOK 2
19	see below	Text Features: Graph	RI.4.7	DOK 2
20	see below	Main Idea and Key Details	RI.4.2	DOK 3
21	see below	Compare Across Texts	W.4.9b	DOK 4
22	A	Sentences Using Prepositions	L.4.1e	DOK 1

Answer Key

Name: _____

Question	Correct Answer	Content Focus	CCSS	Complexity
23	C	Negatives	L.4.1	DOK 1
24	D	Prepositions	L.4.1e	DOK 1
25	D	Sentences Using Prepositions	L.4.1e	DOK 1
26	B	Comparing with Adverbs	L.3.1g	DOK 1
27	C	Prepositions	L.4.1e	DOK 1
28	C	Negatives	L.4.1	DOK 1
29	B	Adverbs	L.4.1a	DOK 1
30	A	Comparing with Adverbs	L.3.1g	DOK 1
31	B	Adverbs	L.4.1a	DOK 1

Comprehension: Selected Response 1, 3, 6A, 6B, 9, 12A, 12B, 13, 16, 19	/16	%
Comprehension: Constructed Response 7, 14, 17, 20, 21	/12	%
Vocabulary 2, 4, 5A, 5B, 8, 10, 11, 15, 18	/16	%
English Language Conventions 22–31	/10	%
Total Unit Assessment Score	/54	%

3. Students should draw lines to match the following:
- Imagery: "Riding in the automobile was quite an experience as cars elbowed past like people at a crowded party."
- Imagery: "The white monster squatting in the corner turned out to be a refrigerator."

4. Students should draw lines to match the following:
- homophones: knew/new
- homophones: made/maid

7. **2-point response:** The author uses imagery to describe what Hattie sees when she visits her relatives in a city. She is experiencing many new sights and sounds, so the author helps the reader understand how different this place is from her home. The paragraph describes the tall brick house with the red front door and the big, soft armchair.

10. Students should draw lines to match the following:
- homophones: knows/nose
- homophones: write/right

14. **2-point response:** Mrs. Henderson shows Emily and Lucas pictures of their relatives and the businesses they ran. This helps both characters better understand their history and how the entire family has been focused on communication. They see pictures of their much younger grandmother working in the store, and then when they hear that their brother has gotten a job selling phones, they how this connects with the family's past.

17. **2-point response:** The main idea of this passage is that the bicycle is an important invention that has been through many changes to become what it is now.

19 Students should draw lines to match the following:
• bicycle structure: A bicycle is presented that has less weight.
• bicycle structure: The tires on bicycles are completely changed.

20 **2-point response:** The most important information about training to be a professional cyclist is that you have to be dedicated to training to reach your goal. Cyclists have to train six days a week at least two hours a day and eat healthy foods like vegetables and protein to develop strong muscles.

21 **4-point response:** The passages show that many people worked to perfect the bicycle over years and years. The bicycle in its early forms was uncomfortable and dangerous. In the early 1800s, both the frame and the wheels were made of wood. There were no pedals, so the rider had to sit on it and push it with his or her feet. These bicycles were called Hobbyhorses. Later, in 1839, Kirkpatrick MacMillan added foot pedals using long rods to connect the rear wheels. About 30 years later, Pierre Michaux and his son Ernst improved the pedals and added a crank to the front wheel. However, it provided a really rough ride, so much so that this design was known as the Boneshaker. Later, in the 1870s, another version of the bicycle was designed. The Penny Farthing had a front wheel five feet high and two small back wheels. These bicycles went very fast but often threw their riders. It wasn't until the 1880s that the front and back wheels were made the same size, which made for a much safer bike and a much smoother ride.

After many improvements and trials, the bicycle is now much more comfortable, stable, and lightweight. Its weight was greatly reduced to make it better for racing. To be good at bicycling you still need strong muscles, but your risk of injury is much lower than before.

Answer Key

Name: _____

Opinion Performance Task				
Question	**Answer**	**CCSS**	**Complexity**	**Score**
1	see below	RI.4.1, RI.4.2, RI.4.3, RI.4.7, RI.4.8, RI.4.9 W.4.1a-d, W.4.4, W.4.7 L.4.1, L.4.2	DOK 3	/1
2	see below		DOK 3	/2
3	see below		DOK 3	/2
Opinion Paper	see below		DOK 4	/4 [P/O] /4 [E/E] /2 [C]
Total Score				**/15**

1 Students should draw lines to match the following:
- Source #1: Many types of fuel used to produce electricity have become more costly and hard to find.
- Source #2: As fossil fuels become harder and more expensive to find, renewable energy sources have become more popular.

2 **2-point response:** Source #2 points out that since fossil fuels are getting more expensive and harder to find, it is essential that people explore renewable energy sources. The main types of renewable energy, including hydropower and geothermal, are explained and shown as ways to help the world's energy reserves.

3 **2-point response:** Source #1, "Energy Efficiency and Conservation," explains that energy is needed to run the world, but that it is getting harder and more expensive to find, so it is essential that people do whatever they can to use less energy, giving tips on how to do so. Source #2, "Renewable Energy Sources," also briefly explains how energy is used in the U.S., but then it focuses on sources that are renewable, and how these sources can provide energy that is less costly and will not run out.

10-point anchor paper: Our school should reduce its energy usage by using efficient appliances and renewable energy sources. It should also educate students about the importance of saving energy. This will help us in many ways. The school will save money, help keep the air clean, and avoid wasting resources that people may need in the future. Also, students will learn to save energy for the rest of our lives.

The first thing our school should do is replace all the light bulbs and appliances with new ones that use less energy. This is an easy step that will save money right away. The school should look for Energy Star stickers on the appliances it buys to make sure the appliances are efficient.

The next thing our school should do is post rules in every classroom to remind everyone to close the windows and doors when the heat or air conditioning is on, open the curtains for sunlight whenever possible, and turn off the lights when leaving the room. The school could even use tools to help students calculate how much energy they are using. This would help us learn how we can make a difference.

The air conditioner is what uses the most electricity in the school. Our school should use renewable resources for this electricity. Renewable resources could be biomass, hydropower, geothermal, wind, or solar power. Biomass energy comes from plants and animals. Hydropower comes from moving water. Geothermal energy comes from inside the earth, and wind and solar power come from the wind and the sun. Our school could use any of those. However, hydropower and geothermal energy can only be used where there are hydropower and geothermal power plants nearby. Wind energy can only be used where there is a wind farm, and even there, only when the wind is blowing. Solar power can only be used when the sun is shining. Since we want to power the air conditioner, solar power would work well because the sun is usually shining when we need the air conditioner. The school should start using solar power.

By switching to renewable energy sources and being more efficient about energy usage, our school can save a lot of money and make the world a better place in the future. It can also teach students how to do a better job of saving energy in other parts of our lives. It is very important that our school should do this to set a good example for how to use energy wisely.